THE ULTIMATE UK KETO DIET FOR BEGINNERS

1200 Savory, Easy and Affordable Keto Diet Recipes for Low-Carb Homemade Meals(with 30-DAY MEAL PLAN) Full Colour Version

THELMA J. LANGLEY

Copyright© 2023 By Thelma J. Langley Rights Reserved

This book is copyright protected. It is only for personal use. You cannot amend, distribute, sell, use, quote or paraphrase any part of the content within this book, without the consent of the author or publisher.

Under no circumstances will any blame or legal responsibility be held against the publisher, or author, for any damages, reparation, or monetary loss due to the information contained within this book, either directly or indirectly.

Disclaimer Notice:

Please note the information contained within this document is for educational and entertainment purposes only. All effort has been executed to present accurate, up to date, reliable, complete information. No warranties of any kind are declared or implied. Readers acknowledge that the author is not engaged in the rendering of legal, financial, medical or professional advice. The content within this book has been derived from various sources. Please consult a licensed professional before attempting any techniques outlined in this book.

By reading this document, the reader agrees that under no circumstances is the author responsible for any losses, direct or indirect, that are incurred as a result of the use of the information contained within this document, including, but not limited to, errors, omissions, or inaccuracies.

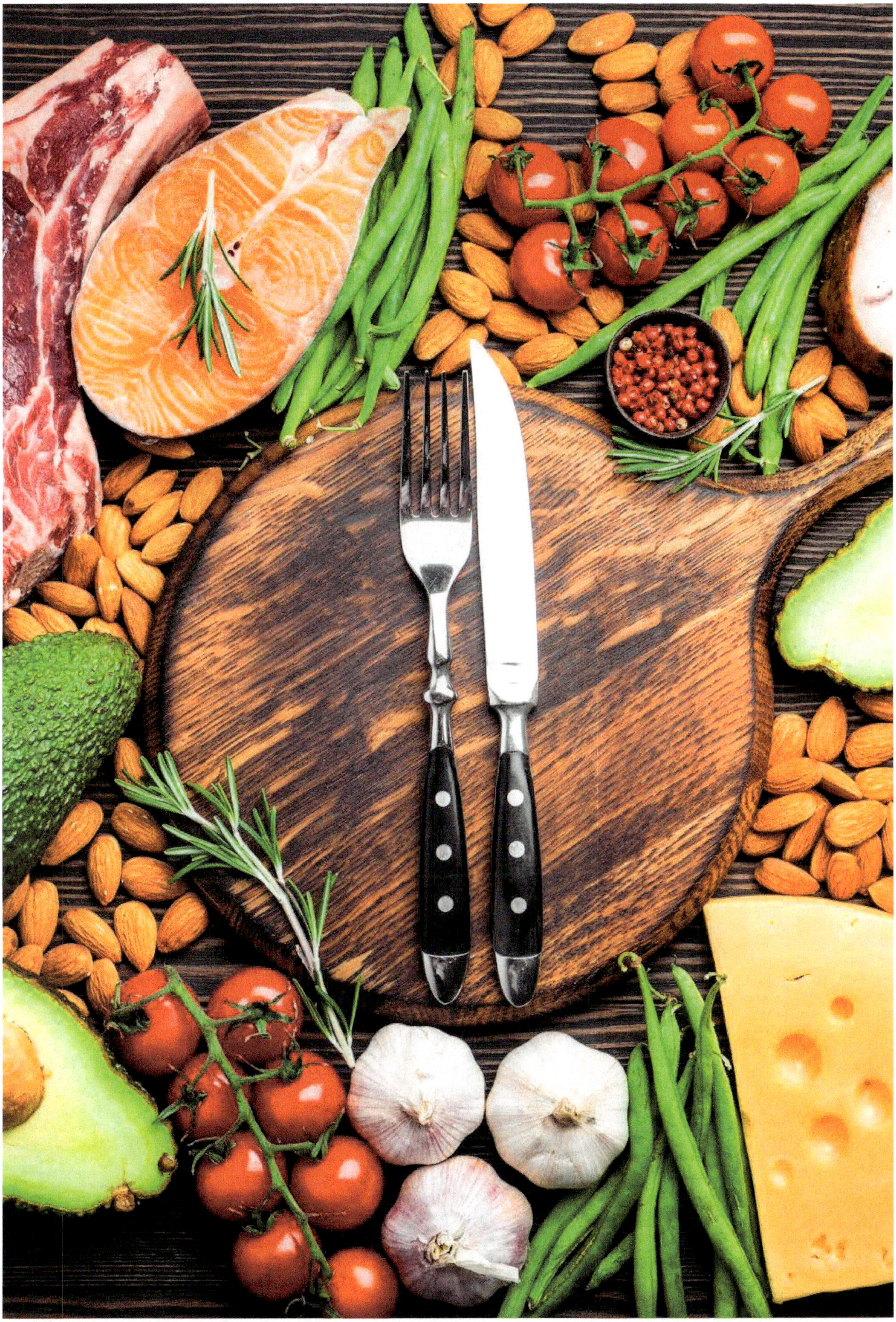

Table of Contents

Introduction	1
Chapter 1	
Basics of Keto Diet	2
Consult with a Healthcare Professional	3
Stock your Kitchen	3
Stay Hydrated	4
Get Support	4
Chapter 2	
Getting Started with the Keto Diet	5
Determine your Macronutrient Needs	6
Plan your Meals and Snacks	6
Be Mindful of your Carbohydrate Intake	6
Chapter 3	
4-Week Meal Plan	8
Week 1	9
Week 2	11
Week 3	13
Week 4	15
Chapter 4	
Breakfast	17
Baked Bacon Egg Cups	18
Breakfast Liver Pate	18
No-Bun Breakfast Bacon Burger	19
Fish Sticks	19
Oregano Fish Sticks	20
Sprouts Hash	20
Breakfast Meatloaf Slices	21
Breakfast Hash	21
Fried Bacon	22
Eggs with Olives	22
Cheddar Biscuits	23
Egg, Bacon and Kale Muffins	23
Eggs with Brussel Sprouts	24
Eggplant Spread	24
Mangalorean Egg Curry	25
Bacon Bites	25
Greens Spread	25
Chapter 5	
Snacks & Appetizers	26
Garlic & Parsley Roasted Mushrooms	27
Ginger & Honey Cauliflower Bites	27
Vegetable Fries	28
Crab & Cheese Soufflé	28
Garlic Brussel Sprouts	29
Lemon Courgette Caviar	29
Hot Pepper Pin Wheel	30
Cheese Zucchini Chips	30
Chocolate Bacon Bites	31
Almond Coconut Granola	31
Deli Turkey and Avocado Roll-Ups	32
Tomato Smokies	32

Pickled Bacon Bowls	33
Turmeric Tempeh	33
Classic Hot Chicken Drumettes	34
Coriander Fennel	34
Banana Peppers Mix	34
Keto "Potato"	35
Anchovies and Cheese Fat Bombs	35
Cheesy Chicken and Ham Bites	36
Cocktail Meatballs with Cheese	36

Chapter 6
Chicken and Poultry — 37

Chicken Kebabs	38
Chicken Bites	38
Tandoori Chicken with Mint Yogurt	38
Coconut Chicken	38
Pesto Chicken	39
Hoisin Chicken	39
Turkey Crust Pizza with Bacon	39
Chicken and Ghee Mix	39
Chicken Wrapped in Bacon	39
Sun-dried Tomatoes and Chicken Mix	40
Chicken Quesadilla Melt	40
Special Chicken Salad	40
Tangy Classic Chicken Drumettes	40
Cumin Chicken Thighs	40
Buttermilk Chicken	41
Cream Cheese Chicken	41
Ranch Chicken Breasts with Cheese	41
Jalapeno Chicken Drumsticks	41
Chicken and Olives Mix	42
Provolone Chicken Breasts	42
Easy Turkey Curry	42
Cheesy Chicken Drumsticks	42

Chapter 7
Beef, Lamb and Pork — 43

Air-Fried Roast Beef	44
Air Fryer Classic Beef Pot Roast	44
Tasty Beef Burgers	44
Onion Carrot Meatloaf	44
Pork with Peppercorn Tomato Sauce	45
Spiced Chops	45
Lemon Pork	45
Pork Cutlets with Spanish Onion	45
Thyme and Turmeric Pork	46
Parmesan Meatballs	46
Sweet & Tangy Meatballs	46
Tender Pork	46
Melt-in-Your-Mouth Pork Roast	47
Vinegar Pork Chops	47
African Style Pork Shoulder	47
Pork Stuffing	47
Dijon Pork Chops	48
Rich and Easy Pork Ragout	48
Chunky Pork Soup with Mustard Greens	48

Chapter 8
Fish and Seafood — 49

Salmon with Dill Sauce	50
Air-Fried Asian Style Fish	50
Chili Haddock	50
Lime Cod	50
Blackened Salmon	50
Tilapia and Kale	51
Mackerel with Spring Onions and Peppers	51
Black Cod with Grapes, Pecans, Fennel & Kale	51
Grilled Salmon with Capers & Dill	51
Cumin Catfish	51
Tender Tilapia	52
Rosemary Shrimp Skewers	52
Pan Fried Garlicky Fish	52

Chapter 9
Vegetarian Recipes — 53

Coconut Chips	54
Sweet Potato Chips	54
Vegetable Spring Rolls	54
Coconut Broccoli	54
Zucchini and Squash Mix	54
Broccoli and Cranberries Mix	55
Onion Pakora	55
Prosciutto Asparagus Mix	55
Cheesy Okra	55
Garlic Fennel Bulb	55
Coconut Kohlrabi Mash	55
Dijon Mustard Asparagus	56
Pecan Spinach	56

Chapter 10
Desserts and Staples — 57

Air-Fried Pineapple in Macadamia Batter	58
Coconut Prune Cookies	58
Delicious Clafoutis	58
Butter Donuts	58
Cinnamon Donuts	59
Almond Donuts	59
Vanilla Pie	59
Creamy Nutmeg Cake	59
Mint Cake	60
Cranberry Whiskey Brownies	60
Vanilla Cookies	60
Raspberry Tart	60
Nutmeg Donuts	61
Soft Turmeric Cookies	61
Coconut Hand Pies	61

Appendix 1 Measurement Conversion Chart — 62
Appendix 2 The Dirty Dozen and Clean Fifteen — 63
Appendix 3 Index — 64

Introduction

Hello everyone! I am your author and thanks for buying my book. It means a lot to me. In this book, I have discussed the keto diet and everything related to the keto diet. You may ask there are plenty of types of diets, but why did you choose the keto diet?

Well, the reason is very personal to me. Growing up I always loved to eat. As a teenager, I used to play sports and exercise. Because of exercising and strong immunity, I did not gain extra weight at that time. But a few years ago, I was gaining weight out of nowhere. It was like everything I am eating is staying in my body. Because of being chunky, my stamina was decreasing day by day. I chose to diet, and after doing different diets I lost a few pounds but it was temporary. After some days I used to gain more weight than before. I was tired due to dieting so I could not do my favorite things.

A friend of mine introduced me to the keto diet and after that day my life changed forever. The Keto diet helped me to lose weight with zero tiredness. To understand how the keto diet works, you have to understand what the keto diet is.

Chapter 1
Basics of Keto Diet

The Keto diet is a low-carb and high-fat diet. Unlike other diets, here you have to cut out carbohydrates and replace them with protein and fat. Our body needs glucose to feed the cells. And glucose comes from carbs. In a keto diet when you cut out the carbs, the body uses fatty acids and ketone bodies for energy. This way the human body burns the stored fat and protein. The average weight loss by the keto diet is 10-12 pounds. This process might look slow but this is good for the body. You do not have to go through weakness and you can continue exercise for betterment.

The keto diet contains 70%-80% fat, 10%-20% protein, and 5%-10% carbohydrate. That means in a 2,000-calorie diet, it's 167 grams of fat, 100 grams of protein, and 25 grams of carbs.

If you have no idea about the keto diet, do not worry. This book is designed especially for newbies. When I started the keto diet, I also did not have enough information about the keto diet, I tried to solve the problems I faced at that time. It will be a perfect guideline for anyone who wants to lose weight on a keto diet.

In this diet book, you will find information related to the keto diet and you will be able to learn many new things. Every recipe comes with its calorie counts so you can calculate how much you are consuming per meal. People have many misconceptions about the keto diet, like diet food does not taste good. It is because people do not have the best guideline, but you have.
This book has all kinds of recipes like eggs, fish, beef, meat, vegetables, and even pork.

I hope that you will find this diet book helpful and share it with your loved ones.

Consult with a Healthcare Professional

It is important to speak with a healthcare professional, such as a registered dietitian or your doctor, before starting any new diet. They can help you determine if a ketogenic diet is safe and appropriate for you, based on your medical history and current health status.

Stock your Kitchen

Stocking your kitchen with keto-friendly foods can make it easier to follow a ketogenic diet. Here are some ideas for foods to include in your kitchen:

Fats: Fats are an important part of a ketogenic diet, as they provide energy and help you feel satisfied. Some good sources of healthy fats include avocados, olive oil, coconut oil, nuts, and seeds.

Protein: Choose high-quality sources of protein such as meat, poultry, fish, and eggs. You can also include small amounts of protein from nuts and seeds, but be mindful of the carbohydrate content.

Low-carb vegetables: Vegetables are an important part of a healthy diet, and they can also help you meet your fiber needs on a ketogenic diet. Choose low-carb vegetables such as leafy greens (spinach, kale, collard greens), broccoli, cauliflower, and bell peppers.

Dairy: Dairy products can be a good source of fat and protein on a ketogenic diet. Choose full-fat options such as cheese, heavy cream, and sour cream.

Condiments: Keep a variety of condiments on hand to add flavor to your meals without adding too many carbs. Some options include olive oil, vinegar, hot sauce, and low-carb salad dressings.

Snacks: Keep a supply of keto-friendly snacks on hand to help you stay on track when you're on the go. Some ideas include nuts, seeds, cheese, hard-boiled eggs, and low-carb protein bars.

By stocking your kitchen with these foods, you'll be well-prepared to follow a ketogenic diet and stay on track with your health goals.

Stay Hydrated

it is important to stay hydrated on a ketogenic diet. When you are in ketosis, your body will excrete more water, so it is important to drink enough fluids to replace what is lost.

Aim to drink at least 8-12 cups of water per day, and consider adding electrolytes to your water to help replenish any lost through increased urination. Good sources of electrolytes include sodium, potassium, and magnesium.

You can also get hydration from other sources such as broth, coconut water, and herbal teas. Be sure to avoid sugary drinks and alcohol, as these can interfere with ketosis and may have negative effects on your health.

Staying hydrated is important for overall health and can help you feel your best on a ketogenic diet. Be sure to drink enough fluids and pay attention to your body's thirst signals to ensure you are getting enough hydration.

Get Support

Starting a new diet can be challenging, so it can be helpful to enlist the support of friends, family, or a healthcare professional. Here are some ways to get support when starting a ketogenic diet:

Talk to your healthcare professional: A healthcare professional, such as a registered dietitian or your doctor, can provide guidance and support as you start a ketogenic diet. They can help you determine if a ketogenic diet is safe and appropriate for you, and provide recommendations for how to follow the diet effectively.

Join a support group: Consider joining a support group or online community to connect with others who are following a ketogenic diet. This can be a great source of motivation and can provide a sense of community and support as you navigate the challenges of starting a new diet.

Seek out resources and education: There are many resources available to help you get started with a ketogenic diet. Consider reading books, following blogs or social media accounts, or watching educational videos to learn more about the diet and how to follow it effectively.

Enlist the support of friends and family: Sharing your goals and progress with friends and family can help provide motivation and accountability as you start a ketogenic diet. They can also offer support and encouragement as you navigate the challenges of starting a new diet.

Consider working with a coach or counselor: If you are struggling with the emotional aspects of starting a new diet, consider working with a coach or counselor who can provide support and guidance. They can help you develop healthy coping mechanisms and provide a safe space to discuss any challenges or struggles you may be facing.

By seeking out support and resources, you can make the process of starting a ketogenic diet easier and more rewarding.

Chapter 2
Getting Started with the Keto Diet

Starting a ketogenic diet can be a bit overwhelming, but it can also be very rewarding if you follow some basic guidelines. Here are some steps to get you started:

Determine your Macronutrient Needs

A ketogenic diet typically consists of high fat, moderate protein, and very low carbohydrate intake. To determine your specific macronutrient needs, you can use a macronutrient calculator or consult with a healthcare professional.

A ketogenic diet typically consists of high fat, moderate protein, and very low carbohydrate intake. The exact ratio of macronutrients that you need will depend on a variety of factors, including your age, gender, weight, height, and activity level.

To use a macronutrient calculator, you will need to enter your age, gender, weight, height, and activity level. The calculator will then provide you with an estimated daily calorie intake, as well as specific macronutrient recommendations for a ketogenic diet.

It is important to note that these recommendations are estimates and may not be exactly right for everyone. It may be necessary to adjust your macronutrient intake based on how your body responds to the diet. If you are unsure about your specific macronutrient needs, it is always a good idea to consult with a healthcare professional.

Here are some general guidelines for macronutrient intake on a ketogenic diet:

Fat: 70-80% of total calories
Protein: 20-25% of total calories
Carbohydrates: 5-10% of total calories (aim for less than 20-50 grams per day)
Keep in mind that these are general guidelines and your specific needs may vary.

Plan your Meals and Snacks

Planning your meals and snacks in advance can help you stay on track with your ketogenic diet.
Planning your meals in advance can help you stay on track with your ketogenic diet. Here are some steps to follow when planning your keto meals:

Determine your daily calorie and macronutrient needs: Use a macronutrient calculator or consult with a healthcare professional to determine your specific calorie and macronutrient needs for a ketogenic diet.

Make a list of keto-friendly foods: Create a list of keto-friendly foods that you enjoy eating, including fats, proteins, and low-carb vegetables.

Plan your meals and snacks: Use your list of keto-friendly foods to plan your meals and snacks for the week. Consider including a variety of foods to ensure you are getting all of the nutrients you need.

Prepare and pack your meals in advance: Consider preparing and packing your meals in advance to make it easier to stay on track with your ketogenic diet. This can be especially helpful when you are on the go or don't have time to cook.

Stay flexible: It's okay to deviate from your meal plan from time to time, especially if you are eating out or in social situations. Just be mindful of your carbohydrate intake and choose keto-friendly options when possible.

Be Mindful of your Carbohydrate Intake

To enter and maintain ketosis, it is important to be mindful of your carbohydrate intake on a ketogenic diet. The goal of a ketogenic diet is to consume very few carbohydrates, typically less than 20-50 grams per day, in order to force the body to use fat as its primary fuel source.

When you consume carbohydrates, your body breaks them down into glucose, which is then used for energy. When you consume very few carbs, your body is forced to use fat for energy instead. This process is known as ketosis, and it can lead to a number of health benefits, including weight loss and improved blood sugar control.

However, to enter and maintain ketosis, it is important to restrict your carbohydrate intake to a very low level. Be mindful of the sources of carbohydrates in your diet, and choose foods that are high in fiber and low in digestible carbs. This can help you reach and maintain ketosis and get the most benefit from your ketogenic diet.

Monitor your ketone levels: There are several ways to monitor your ketone levels when following a ketogenic diet. Here are a few options:

Ketone meters: Ketone meters are devices that allow you to measure the levels of ketones in your blood. To use a ketone meter, you will need to prick your finger with a lancet and place a drop of blood on a test strip. The test strip is then inserted into the ketone meter, which provides a reading of your ketone levels.

ketone test strips: ketone test strips are similar to glucose test strips and can be used to measure the levels of ketones in your urine. To use a ketone test strip, you will need to urinate into a clean container and then dip the test strip into the urine. The test strip will change color to indicate the level of ketones present.

Breath analyzers: Some breath analyzers can measure the levels of ketones in your breath. To use a breath analyzer, you will need to blow into the device, which will then provide a reading of your ketone levels.

Monitoring your ketone levels can be helpful in determining if you are consuming enough fat and restricting enough carbohydrates to reach and maintain ketosis. It is important to note that different methods of measuring ketones may produce slightly different results, so it is a good idea to use the same method consistently.

Chapter 3
4-Week Meal Plan

WEEKLY MEAL PLAN

WEEK OF:

	BREAKFAST	LUNCH	DINNER	SNACKS
SUNDAY				
MONDAY				
TUESDAY				
WEDNESDAY				
THURSDAY				
FRIDAY				
SATURDAY				

Week 1

Here is the following first week's meal plan for the keto diet. Try to follow the plan thoroughly to start getting the benefits of a keto diet.

Meal Plan	Breakfast	Snack	Lunch	Dinner	Snack
Day-1	Baked Bacon Egg Cups	Vegetable Fries (2 servings)	Chicken Kebabs	Coconut Chips	Vegetable Fries (2 servings)
	Calories: 553 | Total Fat: 43.3g | Carbs: 2.3g | Protein: 37.3g	Calories: 42 | Total Fat: 1.3g | Carbs: 2.1g | Protein: 1.4g	Calories: 289 | Total Fat: 11.2g | Carbs: 9.2g | Protein: 14.6g	Calories: 261 | Total Fat: 9.2g | Carbs: 7.3g | Protein: 6.2g	Calories: 42 | Total Fat: 1.3g | Carbs: 2.1g | Protein: 1.4g
Day-2	Breakfast Liver Pate	Garlic Brussel Sprouts (2 servings)	Chicken Bites	Sweet Potato Chips	Lemon Courgette Caviar (2 servings)
	Calories: 173 | Total Fat: 10.8g | Carbs: 2.2g | Protein: 16.1g	Calories: 54 | Fat: 2.5g | Fiber: 2.9g | Carbs: 7.2g | Protein: 2.7g	Calories: 290 | Total Fat: 11.3g | Carbs: 9.2g | Protein: 14.7g	Calories: 253 | Total Fat: 11.2g | Carbs: 8.4g | Protein: 6.5g	Calories: 76 | Total Fat: 0.3g | Carbs: 18g | Protein: 3g
Day-3	No-Bun Breakfast Bacon Burger	Crab & Cheese Soufflé	Coconut Chicken	Vegetable Spring Rolls	Hot Pepper Pin Wheel (2 servings)
	Calories: 618 | Total Fat: 37.8g | Carbs: 8.6g | Protein: 59.4g	Calories: 202 | Total Fat: 5.6g | Carbs: 6.2g | Protein: 14.3g	Calories: 172 | Fat: 6.9g | Fiber: 0.2g | Carbs: 0.5g | Protein: 25.6g	Calories: 263 | Total Fat: 11.2g | Carbs: 8.6g | Protein: 8.2g	Calories: 67 | Total Fat: 2.1g | Carbs: 0.11g | Protein: 3.2g
Day-4	Fish Sticks	Cheese Zucchini Chips (2 servings)	Pesto Chicken	Pork Stuffing	Chocolate Bacon Bites
	Calories: 101 | Fat: 5g | Fiber: 1g | Carbs: 1.9g | Protein: 12.4g	Calories: 127 | Fat: 9.7g | Fiber: 2.1g | Carbs: 5.1g | Protein: 7.3g	Calories: 244 | Fat: 11g | Fiber: 4g | Carbs: 6g | Protein: 17g	Calories: 667 | Fat: 47.9g | Fiber: 1.2g | Carbs: 2.2g | Protein: 54.9g	Calories: 151 | Fat: 4g | Fiber: 2g | Carbs: 4g | Protein: 8g

Day-5	Oregano Fish Sticks	Coconut Prune Cookies	Tasty Beef Burgers	Dijon Pork Chops	Delicious Clafoutis
	Calories: 89 | Fat: 4.3g | Fiber: 0.7g | Carbs: 1.4g | Protein: 11.6g	Calories: 227 | Total Fat: 10.3g | Carbs: 32.5g | Protein: 2.3g	Calories: 302 | Total Fat: 12.3g | Carbs: 11.2g | Protein: 16.4g	Calories: 265 | Fat: 20.6g | Fiber: 0.5g | Carbs: 0.8g | Protein: 18.3g	Calories: 354 | Total Fat: 9.6g | Carbs: 66.6g | Protein: 6.2g
Day-6	Sprouts Hash	Cheese Zucchini Chips (2 servings)	Onion Carrot Meatloaf	Rich and Easy Pork Ragout	Chocolate Bacon Bites
	Calories: 242 | Fat: 12g | Fiber: 3g | Carbs: 5g | Protein: 9g	Calories: 127 | Fat: 9.7g | Fiber: 2.1g | Carbs: 5.1g | Protein: 7.3g	Calories: 306 | Total Fat: 12.7g | Carbs: 12.3g | Protein: 16.8g	Calories: 389 | Fat: 24.3g | Carbs: 5.4g | Total Carbs: 33.1g | Fiber: 1.3g	Calories: 151 | Fat: 4g | Fiber: 2g | Carbs: 4g | Protein: 8g
Day-7	Breakfast Meatloaf Slices	Coconut Prune Cookies	Spiced Chops	Onion Pakora	Delicious Clafoutis
	Calories: 176 | Total Fat: 6.2g | Carbs: 3.4g | Protein: 22.2g	Calories: 227 | Total Fat: 10.3g | Carbs: 32.5g | Protein: 2.3g	Calories: 335 | Fat: 26.7g | Fiber: 0.5g | Carbs: 1.3g | Protein: 21.5g	Calories: 253 | Total Fat: 12.2g | Carbs: 11.4g | Protein: 7.6g	Calories: 354 | Total Fat: 9.6g | Carbs: 66.6g | Protein: 6.2g

Week 2

Here is the following second week's meal plan for a keto diet. It's the second stage of the 4 weeks meal plan that you must take into account carefully.

Meal Plan	Breakfast	Snack	Lunch	Dinner	Snack
Day-1	Egg, Bacon and Kale Muffins	Almond Donuts	Lemon Pork	Chili Haddock	Pickled Bacon Bowls
	Calories: 384 | Fat: 29.8g | Carbs: 5.1g | Protein: 24g | Fiber: 1.1g	Calories: 323 | Fat: 29.4g | Fiber: 4.6g | Carbs: 10g | Protein: 10.5g	Calories: 287 | Fat: 13g | Fiber: 4g | Carbs: 6g | Protein: 20g	Calories: 122 | Fat: 2.8g | Fiber: 0.5g | Carbs: 0.6g | Protein: 22.5g	Calories: 100 | Fat: 4g | Fiber: 2g | Carbs: 3g | Protein: 4g
Day-2	Eggs with Brussel Sprouts	Vanilla Pie (2 servings)	Thyme and Turmeric Pork	Lime Cod	Vanilla Pie
	Calories: 178 | Fat: 9.3g | Fiber: 4.4g | Carbs: 11.4g | Protein: 15g	Calories: 139 | Fat: 8.9g | Fiber: 5.3g | Carbs: 9.5g | Protein: 4.4g	Calories: 170 | Fat: 4.5g | Fiber: 0.5g | Carbs: 0.8g | Protein: 29.8g	Calories: 240 | Fat: 14g | Fiber: 2g | Carbs: 4g | Protein: 16g	Calories: 139 | Fat: 8.9g | Fiber: 5.3g | Carbs: 9.5g | Protein: 4.4g
Day-3	Eggplant Spread	Creamy Nutmeg Cake (2 servings)	Parmesan Meatballs	Blackened Salmon	Turmeric Tempeh (2 servings)
	Calories: 113 | Fat: 1.6g | Fiber: 14.9g | Carbs: 24.8g | Protein: 4.2g	Calories: 81 | Fat: 6.7g | Fiber: 1.1g | Carbs: 3.2g | Protein: 3.4	Calories: 142 | Fat: 5.4g | Fiber: 0g | Carbs: 1.2g | Protein: 20.8g	Calories: 201 | Fat: 9.9g | Fiber: 0.4g | Carbs: 0.9g | Protein: 27.8g	Calories: 87 | Fat: 5g | Fiber: 0.2g | Carbs: 4.3g | Protein: 7.9g
Day-4	Mangalorean Egg Curry	Mint Cake	Sweet & Tangy Meatballs	Tilapia and Kale	Mint Cake
	Calories: 305 | Fat: 16.4g | Carbs: 5.7g | Protein: 32.2g | Fiber: 1.1g	Calories: 538 | Fat: 48.5g | Fiber: 6.9g | Carbs: 14.1g | Protein: 20.8g	Calories: 298 | Total Fat: 12.2g | Carbs: 11.6g | Protein: 15.8g	Calories: 240 | Fat: 12g | Fiber: 2g | Carbs: 4g | Protein: 12g	Calories: 538 | Fat: 48.5g | Fiber: 6.9g | Carbs: 14.1g | Protein: 20.8g

Day-5	Bacon Bites	Coriander Fennel (2 servings)	Tender Pork	Grilled Salmon with Capers & Dill	Raspberry Tart (2 servings)
	Calories: 397 | Fat: 30.8g | Fiber: 0.2g | Carbs: 1.5g | Protein: 26.6g	Calories: 40 | Fat: 0.7g | Fiber: 3.7g | Carbs: 8.5g | Protein: 1.2g	Calories: 808 | Fat: 59.4g | Fiber: 0.3g | Carbs: 0.6g | Protein: 63.6g	Calories: 300 | Total Fat: 8.9g | Carbs: 7.3g | Protein: 16.2g	Calories: 96 | Fat: 9.2g | Fiber: 0.8g | Carbs: 1.9g | Protein: 2.4g
Day-6	Greens Spread	Banana Peppers Mix	Melt-in-Your-Mouth Pork Roast	Dijon Mustard Asparagus	Banana Peppers Mix (2 servings)
	Calories: 100 | Fat: 7.2g | Fiber: 1.2g | Carbs: 2.5g | Protein: 7.6g	Calories: 133 | Fat: 10.1g | Fiber: 1.1g | Carbs: 2.9g | Protein: 8.2g	Calories: 497 | Fat: 35.3g | Carbs: 2.5g | Total Carbs: 40.2g | Fiber: 0.6g	Calories: 58 | Fat: 4g | Fiber: 2.7g | Carbs: 4.9g | Protein: 2.8g	Calories: 133 | Fat: 10.1g | Fiber: 1.1g | Carbs: 2.9g | Protein: 8.2g
Day-7	Breakfast Liver Pate	Keto "Potato" (2 servings)	Vinegar Pork Chops	Pecan Spinach	Tomato Smokies
	Calories: 173 | Total Fat: 10.8g | Carbs: 2.2g | Protein: 16.1g	Calories: 80 | Fat: 4g | Fiber: 2.8g | Carbs: 6.2g | Protein: 6.6g	Calories: 271 | Fat: 21.1g | Fiber: 0.1g | Carbs: 0.5g | Protein: 18g	Calories: 82 | Fat: 8.5g | Fiber: 1.1g | Carbs: 1.5g | Protein: 1.2g	Calories: 126 | Fat: 9.7g | Fiber: 0.1g | Carbs: 1.4g | Protein: 8.7g

Week 3

Here is the following third week's meal plan for a keto diet. In this stage, you already got the result of the previous two weeks' diet plan. So, follow this third stage of the meal plan completely to get a better result.

Meal Plan	Breakfast	Snack	Lunch	Dinner	Snack
Day-1	Breakfast Hash	Garlic & Parsley Roasted Mushrooms (2 servings)	Air-Fried Roast Beef	Chicken and Olives Mix	Chocolate Bacon Bites
	Calories: 445 | Total Fat: 36.1g | Carbs: 3.5g | Protein: 26.3g	Calories: 92 | Total Fat: 0.23g | Carbs: 0.52g | Protein: 1.2g	Calories: 304 | Total Fat: 12.8g | Carbs: 11.7g | Protein: 16.8g	Calories: 270 | Fat: 14g | Fiber: 4g | Carbs: 6g | Protein: 18g	Calories: 151 | Fat: 4g | Fiber: 2g | Carbs: 4g | Protein: 8g
Day-2	Breakfast Liver Pate	Ginger & Honey Cauliflower Bites (2 servings)	Lime Cod	Chicken Bites	Delicious Clafoutis
	Calories: 173 | Total Fat: 10.8g | Carbs: 2.2g | Protein: 16.1g	Calories: 42 | Total Fat: 2.3g | Carbs: 3.1g | Protein: 3.2g	Calories: 240 | Fat: 14g | Fiber: 2g | Carbs: 4g | Protein: 16g	Calories: 290 | Total Fat: 11.3g | Carbs: 9.2g | Protein: 14.7g	Calories: 354 | Total Fat: 9.6g | Carbs: 66.6g | Protein: 6.2
Day-3	Fried Bacon	Garlic Brussel Sprouts (2 servings)	Blackened Salmon	Coconut Chicken	Garlic & Parsley Roasted Mushrooms (2 servings)
	Calories: 537 | Fat: 39.4g | Fiber: 0.1g | Carbs: 1.4g | Protein: 42.7g	Calories: 54 | Fat: 2.5g | Fiber: 2.9g | Carbs: 7.2g | Protein: 2.7g	Calories: 201 | Fat: 9.9g | Fiber: 0.4g | Carbs: 0.9g | Protein: 27.8g	Calories: 172 | Fat: 6.9g | Fiber: 0.2g | Carbs: 0.5g | Protein: 25.6g	Calories: 92 | Total Fat: 0.23g | Carbs: 0.52g | Protein: 1.2g
Day-4	Fish Sticks	Delicious Clafoutis	Tilapia and Kale	Coconut Chips	Delicious Clafoutis
	Calories: 101 | Fat: 5g | Fiber: 1g | Carbs: 1.9g | Protein: 12.4g	Calories: 354 | Total Fat: 9.6g | Carbs: 66.6g | Protein: 6.2g	Calories: 240 | Fat: 12g | Fiber: 2g | Carbs: 4g | Protein: 12g	Calories: 261 | Total Fat: 9.2g | Carbs: 7.3g | Protein: 6.2g	Calories: 354 | Total Fat: 9.6g | Carbs: 66.6g | Protein: 6.2g
Day-5	Eggs with Olives (2 servings)	Banana Peppers Mix	Air Fryer Classic Beef Pot Roast	Tasty Beef Burgers	Banana Peppers Mix

		Calories: 68 | Fat: 4.8g | Fiber: 0.2g | Carbs: 0.7g | Protein: 5.6g	Calories: 133 | Fat: 10.1g | Fiber: 1.1g | Carbs: 2.9g | Protein: 8.2g	Calories: 303 | Total Fat: 12.6g | Carbs: 11.3g | Protein: 16.4g	Calories: 302 | Total Fat: 12.3g | Carbs: 11.2g | Protein: 16.4g	Calories: 133 | Fat: 10.1g | Fiber: 1.1g | Carbs: 2.9g | Protein: 8.2g
Day-6	Sprouts Hash	Anchovies and Cheese Fat Bombs	Dijon Mustard Asparagus	Onion Carrot Meatloaf	Anchovies and Cheese Fat Bombs
	Calories: 242 | Fat: 12g | Fiber: 3g | Carbs: 5g | Protein: 9g	Calories: 391 | Fat: 26.6g | Carbs: 3.1g | Protein: 33.8g | Fiber: 0.7g	Calories: 58 | Fat: 4g | Fiber: 2.7g | Carbs: 4.9g | Protein: 2.8g	Calories: 306 | Total Fat: 12.7g | Carbs: 12.3g | Protein: 16.8g	Calories: 391 | Fat: 26.6g | Carbs: 3.1g | Protein: 33.8g | Fiber: 0.7g
Day-7	Cheddar Biscuits	Cheesy Chicken and Ham Bites	Air Fryer Classic Beef Pot Roast	Tasty Beef Burgers	Cocktail Meatballs with Cheese
	Calories: 144 | Fat: 9.2g | Fiber: 6.1g | Carbs: 10.9g | Protein: 5.4g	Calories: 289 | Fat: 11.1g | Carbs: 7.2g | Protein: 36.8g | Fiber: 2g	Calories: 303 | Total Fat: 12.6g | Carbs: 11.3g | Protein: 16.4g	Calories: 302 | Total Fat: 12.3g | Carbs: 11.2g | Protein: 16.4g	Calories: 247 | Fat: 18g | Carbs: 1.1g | Protein: 19.1g | Fiber: 0.1g

Week 4

This is the final stage of our 4 week's keto diet meal plan. In this stage, you already have formed a habit of maintaining a keto diet. So, follow this final stage to get best the best result in your body and mind.

Meal Plan	Breakfast	Snack	Lunch	Dinner	Snack
Day-1	Oregano Fish Sticks	Garlic Brussel Sprouts (2 servings)	Chicken Bites	Lemon Pork	Banana Peppers Mix (2 servings)
	Calories: 89 | Fat: 4.3g | Fiber: 0.7g | Carbs: 1.4g | Protein: 11.6g	Calories: 54 | Fat: 2.5g | Fiber: 2.9g | Carbs: 7.2g | Protein: 2.7g	Calories: 290 | Total Fat: 11.3g | Carbs: 9.2g | Protein: 14.7g	Calories: 287 | Fat: 13g | Fiber: 4g | Carbs: 6g | Protein: 20g	Calories: 133 | Fat: 10.1g | Fiber: 1.1g | Carbs: 2.9g | Protein: 8.2g
Day-2	Eggs with Brussel Sprouts	Vanilla Pie	Sweet Potato Chips	Vinegar Pork Chops	Tomato Smokies (2 servings)
	Calories: 178 | Fat: 9.3g | Fiber: 4.4g | Carbs: 11.4g | Protein: 15g	Calories: 139 | Fat: 8.9g | Fiber: 5.3g | Carbs: 9.5g | Protein: 4.4g	Calories: 253 | Total Fat: 11.2g | Carbs: 8.4g | Protein: 6.5g	Calories: 271 | Fat: 21.1g | Fiber: 0.1g | Carbs: 0.5g | Protein: 18g	Calories: 126 | Fat: 9.7g | Fiber: 0.1g | Carbs: 1.4g | Protein: 8.7g
Day-3	Eggplant Spread	Creamy Nutmeg Cake (2 servings)	Vegetable Spring Rolls	Parmesan Meatballs	Chocolate Bacon Bites
	Calories: 113 | Fat: 1.6g | Fiber: 14.9g | Carbs: 24.8g | Protein: 4.2g	Calories: 81 | Fat: 6.7g | Fiber: 1.1g | Carbs: 3.2g | Protein: 3.4g	Calories: 263 | Total Fat: 11.2g | Carbs: 8.6g | Protein: 8.2g	Calories: 142 | Fat: 5.4g | Fiber: 0g | Carbs: 1.2g | Protein: 20.8g	Calories: 151 | Fat: 4g | Fiber: 2g | Carbs: 4g | Protein: 8g
Day-4	Sprouts Hash	Mint Cake	Pork Stuffing	Tilapia and Kale	Vegetable Fries (2 servings)
	Calories: 242 | Fat: 12g | Fiber: 3g | Carbs: 5g | Protein: 9g	Calories: 538 | Fat: 48.5g | Fiber: 6.9g | Carbs: 14.1g | Protein: 20.8g	Calories: 667 | Fat: 47.9g | Fiber: 1.2g | Carbs: 2.2g | Protein: 54.9g	Calories: 240 | Fat: 12g | Fiber: 2g | Carbs: 4g | Protein: 12g	Calories: 42 | Total Fat: 1.3g | Carbs: 2.1g | Protein: 1.4g
Day-5	Bacon Bites	Banana Peppers Mix	Chicken Bites	Tender Pork	Lemon Courgette Caviar (2 servings)
	Calories: 397 | Fat: 30.8g | Fiber: 0.2g | Carbs: 1.5g | Protein: 26.6g	Calories: 133 | Fat: 10.1g | Fiber: 1.1g | Carbs: 2.9g | Protein: 8.2g	Calories: 290 | Total Fat: 11.3g | Carbs: 9.2g | Protein: 14.7g	Calories: 808 | Fat: 59.4g | Fiber: 0.3g | Carbs: 0.6g | Protein: 63.6g	Calories: 76 | Total Fat: 0.3g | Carbs: 18g | Protein: 3g
Day-6	Breakfast Meatloaf Slices	Tomato Smokies (2 servings)	Rich and Easy Pork Ragout	Melt-in-Your-Mouth Pork Roast	Almond Donuts

	Calories: 176 | Total Fat: 6.2g | Carbs: 3.4g | Protein: 22.2g	Calories: 126 | Fat: 9.7g | Fiber: 0.1g | Carbs: 1.4g | Protein: 8.7g	Calories: 389 | Fat: 24.3g | Carbs: 5.4g | Total Carbs: 33.1g | Fiber: 1.3g	Calories: 497 | Fat: 35.3g | Carbs: 2.5g | Total Carbs: 40.2g | Fiber: 0.6g	Calories: 323 | Fat: 29.4g | Fiber: 4.6g | Carbs: 10g | Protein: 10.5g
Day-7	Breakfast Liver Pate	Chocolate Bacon Bites	Thyme and Turmeric Pork	Lime Cod	Vanilla Pie (2 servings)
	Calories: 173 | Total Fat: 10.8g | Carbs: 2.2g | Protein: 16.1g	Calories: 151 | Fat: 4g | Fiber: 2g | Carbs: 4g | Protein: 8g	Calories: 170 | Fat: 4.5g | Fiber: 0.5g | Carbs: 0.8g | Protein: 29.8g	Calories: 240 | Fat: 14g | Fiber: 2g | Carbs: 4g | Protein: 16g	Calories: 139 | Fat: 8.9g | Fiber: 5.3g | Carbs: 9.5g | Protein: 4.4g

Chapter 4
Breakfast

Baked Bacon Egg Cups

Prep Time: 5 minutes | Cook Time: 12 minutes | Serves 2

- 2 eggs
- 1 tablespoon chives, fresh, chopped
- ½ teaspoon paprika
- ½ teaspoon cayenne pepper
- 3-ounces cheddar cheese, shredded
- ½ teaspoon butter
- ¼ teaspoon salt
- 4-ounces bacon, cut into tiny pieces

1. Slice bacon into tiny pieces and sprinkle it with cayenne pepper, salt, and paprika. Mix the chopped bacon. Spread butter in bottom of ramekin dishes and beat the eggs there. Add the chives and shredded cheese. Add the chopped bacon over egg mixture in ramekin dishes.
2. Place the ramekins in your air fryer basket. Preheat your air fryer to 360°Fahrenheit. Place the air fryer basket in your air fryer and cook for 12-minutes. When the cook time is completed, remove the ramekins from air fryer and serve warm.

PER SERVING
Calories: 553 | Total Fat: 43.3g | Carbs: 2.3g | Protein: 37.3g

Breakfast Liver Pate

Prep Time: 5 minutes | Cook Time: 10 minutes | Serves 7

- 1 lb. chicken liver
- 1 teaspoon salt
- ½ teaspoon cilantro, dried
- 1 yellow onion, diced
- 1 teaspoon ground black pepper
- 1 cup water
- 4 tablespoons butter

1. Chop the chicken liver roughly and place it in the air fryer basket tray. Add water to air fryer basket tray and add diced onion.
2. Preheat your air fryer to 360°Fahrenheit and cook chicken liver for 10-minutes. When it is finished cooking, drain the chicken liver. Transfer the chicken liver to blender, add butter, ground black pepper and dried cilantro and blend. Once you get a pate texture, transfer to liver pate bowl and serve immediately or keep in the fridge for later.

PER SERVING
Calories: 173 | Total Fat: 10.8g | Carbs: 2.2g | Protein: 16.1g

No-Bun Breakfast Bacon Burger

Prep Time: 5 minutes | Cook Time: 8 minutes | Serves 2

- 8-ounces ground beef
- 2-ounces lettuce leaves
- ½ teaspoon minced garlic
- 1 teaspoon olive oil
- ½ teaspoon sea salt
- 1 teaspoon ground black pepper
- 1 teaspoon butter
- 4-ounces bacon, cooked
- 1 egg
- ½ yellow onion, diced
- ½ cucumber, slice finely
- ½ tomato, slice finely

1. Begin by whisking the egg in a bowl, then add the ground beef and combine well. Add cooked, chopped bacon to the ground beef mixture. Add butter, ground black pepper, minced garlic, and salt. Mix and make burgers.
2. Preheat your air fryer to 370°Fahrenheit. Spray the air fryer basket with olive oil and place the burgers inside of it. Cook the burgers for 8-minutes on each side. Meanwhile, slice the cucumber, onion, and tomato finely. Place the tomato, onion, and cucumber onto the lettuce leaves. When the burgers are cooked, allow them to chill at room temperature, and place them over the vegetables and serve.

PER SERVING

Calories: 618 | Total Fat: 37.8g | Carbs: 8.6g | Protein: 59.4g

Fish Sticks

Prep Time: 15 minutes | Cook Time: 10 minutes | Serves 4

- 8 oz cod fillet
- 1 egg, beaten
- ¼ cup coconut flour
- ¼ teaspoon ground coriander
- ¼ teaspoon ground paprika
- ¼ teaspoon ground cumin
- ¼ teaspoon Pink salt
- 1/3 cup coconut flakes
- 1 tablespoon mascarpone
- 1 teaspoon heavy cream
- Cooking spray

1. Chop the cod fillet roughly and put it in the blender. Add egg, coconut flour ground coriander, paprika, cumin, salt, and blend the mixture until smooth. After this, transfer it in the bowl.
2. Line the chopping board with parchment. Place the fish mixture over the parchment and flatten it in the shape of the flat square. Then cut the fish square into sticks. In the separated bowl whisk together heavy cream and mascarpone. Sprinkle every fish stick with mascarpone mixture and after this, coat in the coconut flakes.
3. Preheat the air fryer to 400F. Spray the air fryer basket with cooking spray and arrange the fish sticks inside. Cook the fish sticks for 10 minutes. Flip them on another side in halfway of cooking.

PER SERVING

Calories: 101 | Fat: 5g | Fiber: 1g | Carbs: 1.9g | Protein: 12.4g

Oregano Fish Sticks

Prep Time: 15 minutes | Cook Time: 10 minutes | Serves 4

- 8 oz cod fillet
- 1 egg, beaten
- 2 tablespoons coconut shred
- 1 teaspoon dried oregano
- ½ teaspoon salt
- 1 teaspoon avocado oil

1. Cut the cod fillet into sticks.
2. Then mix salt with dried oregano and coconut shred.
3. Dip the cod sticks in the beaten egg and coat in the coconut shred mixture.
4. Sprinkle the cod sticks with avocado oil and cook in the air fryer at 400F for 10 minutes.

PER SERVING

Calories: 89 | Fat: 4.3g | Fiber: 0.7g | Carbs: 1.4g | Protein: 11.6g

Sprouts Hash

Prep Time: 5 minutes | Cook Time: 20 minutes | Serves 4

- 1 tablespoon olive oil
- 1 pound Brussels sprouts, shredded
- 4 eggs, whisked
- ½ cup coconut cream
- Salt and black pepper to the taste
- 1 tablespoon chives, chopped
- ¼ cup cheddar cheese, shredded

1. Preheat the Air Fryer at 360 degrees F and grease it with the oil. Spread the Brussels sprouts on the bottom of the fryer, then add the eggs mixed with the rest of the ingredients, toss a bit and cook for 20 minutes. Divide between plates and serve.

PER SERVING

Calories: 242 | Fat: 12g | Fiber: 3g | Carbs: 5g | Protein: 9g

Breakfast Meatloaf Slices

Prep Time: 7 minutes | Cook Time: 20 minutes | Serves 6

- 8-ounces ground pork
- 7-ounces ground beef
- 1 teaspoon olive oil
- 1 teaspoon butter
- 1 tablespoon oregano, dried
- 1 teaspoon cayenne pepper
- 1 teaspoon salt
- 1 tablespoon chives
- 1 tablespoon almond flour
- 1 egg
- 1 onion, diced

1. Beat egg in a bowl. Add the ground beef and ground pork. Add the chives, almond flour, cayenne pepper, salt, dried oregano, and butter. Add diced onion to ground beef mixture. Use hands to shape a meatloaf mixture.
2. Preheat the air fryer to 350°Fahrenheit. Spray the inside of the air fryer basket with olive oil and place the meatloaf inside it. Cook the meatloaf for 20-minutes. When the meatloaf has cooked, allow it to chill for a bit. Slice and serve it.

PER SERVING
Calories: 176 | Total Fat: 6.2g | Carbs: 3.4g | Protein: 22.2g

Breakfast Hash

Prep Time: 5 minutes | Cook Time: 8 minutes | Serves 4

- 7-ounces bacon, cooked
- 1 zucchini, cubed into small pieces
- 4-ounces cheddar cheese, shredded
- 2 tablespoons butter
- 1 teaspoon ground thyme
- 1 teaspoon cilantro
- 1 teaspoon paprika
- 1 teaspoon ground black pepper
- 1 teaspoon salt

1. Chop the zucchini into small cubes and sprinkle with ground black pepper, salt, paprika, cilantro and ground thyme. Preheat your air fryer to 400°Fahrenheit. Add butter to the air fryer basket tray. Melt the butter and add the zucchini cubes. Cook the zucchini cubes for 5-minutes.
2. Meanwhile, shred the cheddar cheese. Add the bacon to the zucchini cubes. Sprinkle the zucchini mixture with shredded cheese and cook for 3-minutes more. When cooking is completed, transfer the breakfast hash into serving bowls.

PER SERVING
Calories: 445 | Total Fat: 36.1g | Carbs: 3.5g | Protein: 26.3g

Fried Bacon

Prep Time: 10 minutes | **Cook Time:** 12 minutes | **Serves 4**

- 10 oz bacon
- 3 oz pork rinds
- 2 eggs, beaten
- ½ teaspoon salt
- ½ teaspoon ground black pepper
- Cooking spray

1. Cut the bacon into 4 cubes and sprinkle with salt and ground black pepper. After this dip the bacon cubes in the beaten eggs and coat in the pork rinds. Preheat the air fryer to 395F. Spray the air fryer basket with cooking spray and put the bacon cubes inside. Cook them for 6 minutes. Then flip the bacon on another side and cook for 6 minutes more or until it is light brown.

PER SERVING
Calories: 537 | Fat: 39.4g | Fiber: 0.1g | Carbs: 1.4g | Protein: 42.7g

Eggs with Olives

Prep Time: 5 minutes | **Cook Time:** 20 minutes | **Serves 4**

- 4 eggs, beaten
- 2 Kalamata olives, sliced
- 1 teaspoon avocado oil
- ½ teaspoon ground paprika

1. Brush the air fryer basket with avocado oil and pour the eggs inside.
2. Sprinkle the eggs with ground paprika and top with olives.
3. Bake the meal at 360F for 20 minutes.

PER SERVING
Calories: 68 | Fat: 4.8g | Fiber: 0.2g | Carbs: 0.7g | Protein: 5.6g

Cheddar Biscuits

Prep Time: 15 minutes | Cook Time: 8 minutes | Serves 4

- ½ cup coconut flour
- ¼ cup Cheddar cheese, shredded
- 1 egg, beaten
- 1 tablespoon cream cheese
- 1 tablespoon coconut oil, melted
- ¾ teaspoon baking powder
- ½ teaspoon ground cardamom

1. Mix all ingredients in the mixing bowl and knead the dough.
2. Then make 4 biscuits and put them in the air fryer.
3. Cook the meal at 390F for 8 minutes. Shake the biscuits from time to time to avoid burning.

PER SERVING

Calories: 144 | Fat: 9.2g | Fiber: 6.1g | Carbs: 10.9g | Protein: 5.4g

Egg, Bacon and Kale Muffins

Prep Time: 10 minutes | Cook Time: 25 minutes | Serves 4

- 1/2 cup bacon
- 1 shallot, chopped
- 1 garlic clove, minced
- 1 cup kale
- 1 ripe tomato, chopped
- 6 eggs
- 1 cup Asiago cheese, shredded
- Salt and black pepper, to taste
- 1 teaspoon dried rosemary
- 1/2 teaspoon dried basil
- 1/2 teaspoon dried marjoram

1. Start by preheating your oven to 390 degrees F. Add muffin liners to a muffin tin.
2. Preheat your pan over medium heat. Cook the bacon for 3 to 4 minutes; now, chop the bacon and reserve.

PER SERVING

Calories: 384 | Fat: 29.8g | Carbs: 5.1g | Protein: 24g | Fiber: 1.1g

Eggs with Brussel Sprouts

Prep Time: 5 minutes | Cook Time: 20 minutes | Serves 4

- 1-pound Brussel sprouts, shredded
- 8 eggs, beaten
- 1 teaspoon avocado oil
- 1 teaspoon ground turmeric
- ½ teaspoon salt

1. Mix all ingredients and stir until homogenous.
2. Pour the mixture in the air fryer basket and cook at 365F for 20 minutes.

PER SERVING

Calories: 178 | Fat: 9.3g | Fiber: 4.4g | Carbs: 11.4g | Protein: 15g

Eggplant Spread

Prep Time: 15 minutes | Cook Time: 20 minutes | Serves 4

- 3 eggplants
- 1 teaspoon chili flakes
- 1 teaspoon salt
- ½ teaspoon ground black pepper
- 2 tablespoons avocado oil

1. Peel the eggplants and rub them with salt.
2. Cook the eggplants in the air fryer at 365F for 20 minutes.
3. Then chop the eggplant and put it in the blender.
4. Add all remaining ingredients and blend the mixture until smooth.

PER SERVING

Calories: 113 | Fat: 1.6g | Fiber: 14.9g | Carbs: 24.8g | Protein: 4.2g

Mangalorean Egg Curry

Prep Time: 5 minutes | Cook Time: 20 minutes | Serves 4

- 2 tablespoons rice bran oil
- 1/2 cup scallions, chopped
- 1 teaspoon Kashmiri chili powder
- 1/4 teaspoon carom seeds
- 1/4 teaspoon methi seeds
- Kosher salt and ground black pepper, to taste
- 2 ripe tomatoes, pureed
- 2 teaspoons tamarind paste
- 1/2 cup chicken stock
- 4 boiled egg, peeled
- 1 teaspoon curry paste
- 2 tablespoons curry leaves
- 1/2 teaspoon cinnamon powder
- 1/2 cup coconut milk
- 1 tablespoon cilantro leaves

1. Heat the oil in a pan over medium heat. Now, cook the scallions and chili until tender and fragrant.
2. Add carom seeds, methi seeds, salt, pepper, and tomatoes; cook for a further 8 minutes.
3. Then, add the tamarind paste and chicken stock. Reduce the heat to medium-low and cook for 3 minutes more.
4. Add the eggs, curry paste, curry leaves, cinnamon powder, and coconut milk. Let it simmer for 6 minutes more. Garnish with cilantro leaves. Bon appétit!

PER SERVING

Calories: 305 | Fat: 16.4g | Carbs: 5.7g | Protein: 32.2g | Fiber: 1.1g

Bacon Bites

Prep Time: 10 minutes | Cook Time: 12 minutes | Serves 4

- 10 oz bacon, chopped
- 1 teaspoon dried dill
- 4 teaspoons cream cheese
- 1 teaspoon dried oregano

1. Put the bacon in the air fryer in one layer and bake for 12 minutes at 375F. Shake the bacon from time to time to avoid burning.
2. Then mix bacon with remaining ingredients and make the balls (bites)
3. Now, cook the shallots and garlic in the bacon fat until they are tender. Add the remaining ingredients and mix to combine well.
4. Pour the batter into muffin cups and bake for 13 minutes or until the edges are slightly browned.
5. Allow your muffins to stand for 5 minutes before removing from the tin. Bon appétit!

PER SERVING

Calories: 397 | Fat: 30.8g | Fiber: 0.2g | Carbs: 1.5g | Protein: 26.6g

Greens Spread

Prep Time: 5 minutes | Cook Time: 10 minutes | Serves 4

- 2 tablespoons heavy cream
- 3 cups arugula, chopped
- 2 tablespoons dried oregano
- 1 oz pork rinds
- 1 oz Parmesan, grated

1. Mix all ingredients in the air fryer basket and cook them at 365F for 10 minutes.
2. Then carefully mix the cooked mixture again and blend with the help of the immersion blender to get the spread texture.

PER SERVING

Calories: 100 | Fat: 7.2g | Fiber: 1.2g | Carbs: 2.5g | Protein: 7.6g

Chapter 5
Snacks & Appetizers

Garlic & Parsley Roasted Mushrooms

Prep Time: 10 minutes | Cook Time: 30 minutes | Serves 4

- 2 lbs. mushrooms, washed, quartered, dried
- 1 tablespoon duck fat
- ½ teaspoon garlic powder
- 2 teaspoons Herbes de Provence
- 2 tablespoons white vermouth
- 1 teaspoon parsley, fresh, finely chopped

1. Place the duck fat, garlic powder, Herbes de Provence in an air fryer pan and heat for 2-minutes. Stir in the mushrooms. Cook for 25-minutes at 300°Fahrenheit.
2. Mix in the vermouth and cook for an additional 5-minutes. Sprinkle mushrooms with parsley for garnish.

PER SERVING

Calories: 92 | Total Fat: 0.23g | Carbs: 0.52g | Protein: 1.2g

Ginger & Honey Cauliflower Bites

Prep Time: 5 minutes | Cook Time: 20 minutes | Serves 4

- 1 head of cauliflower, cut into florets
- 1/3 cup oats
- 1/3 cup almond flour
- 1 egg, beaten
- 1 teaspoon mixed spice
- 2 tablespoons soy sauce
- 2 tablespoons honey
- Salt and pepper to taste
- ½ teaspoon mustard powder
- 1 teaspoon mixed herbs
- 1/3 cup desiccated coconut
- 1 teaspoon ginger powder

1. Preheat your air fryer to 360°Fahrenheit. In a bowl, combine flour, oats, ginger powder and coconut. Season it with salt and pepper. Add egg into another bowl. Season the cauliflower florets with the mixed herbs, salt, and pepper. Dip florets into the egg and then dredge in coconut mix.
2. Cook in your air fryer for 15-minutes at 315°Fahrenheit. Mix remaining ingredients in a bowl. Dip the cauliflower in the honey mixture and cook for an additional 5-minutes in air fryer.

PER SERVING

Calories: 42 | Total Fat: 2.3g | Carbs: 3.1g | Protein: 3.2g

Vegetable Fries
Prep Time: 5 minutes | Cook Time: 18 minutes | Serves 4

- 5-ounces sweet potatoes, peeled and chopped as chips
- 5-ounces Courgette, peeled and chopped as chips
- 5-ounces carrots, peeled and chopped as chips
- 2 tablespoons olive oil
- Salt and pepper to taste
- Pinch of basil
- Pinch of mixed spice

1. Toss the veggies in olive oil and place in an air fryer preheated to 360°Fahrenehit for 18-minutes. Toss twice during cook time. Season with salt, pepper, and other seasonings.

PER SERVING
Calories: 42 | Total Fat: 1.3g | Carbs: 2.1g | Protein: 1.4g

Crab & Cheese Soufflé
Prep Time: 5 minutes | Cook Time: 18 minutes | Serves 2

- 1 lb. cooked crab meat
- 1 capsicum
- 1 small onion, diced
- 1 cup cream
- 1 cup milk
- 4-ounces Brie
- Brandy to cover crab meat
- 3 eggs
- 5 drops liquid stevia
- 3-ounces cheddar cheese, grated
- 4 cups bread, cubed

1. Soak the cram meat in brandy and 4-parts water. Loosen the meat in brandy. Sauté onion and bread. Grate cheddar cheese and mix ingredients. In the same pan, add some of the butter and stir for a minute. Add the crab to pan. Add ½ of the milk and 1 tablespoon of brandy and cook for 2-minutes.
2. Add the bread cubes to frying pan and mix well. Sprinkle with cheese and pepper. Put the stuffing in 5 ramekins, without brushing them with oil. Distribute the brie evenly. In a bowl, combine ½ cup of cream with stevia. Heat the cream in a pan and add remaining milk. Pour mixture into ramekins. Preheat your air fryer to 350°Fahreneheit add dish and cook for 20-minutes.

PER SERVING
Calories: 202 | Total Fat: 5.6g | Carbs: 6.2g | Protein: 14.3g

Garlic Brussel Sprouts

Prep Time: 10 minutes | Cook Time: 13 minutes | Serves 6

- pound Brussel sprouts
- 1 teaspoon garlic powder
- 1 teaspoon ground coriander
- 1 tablespoon coconut oil
- 1 tablespoon apple cider vinegar

1. Put coconut oil in the air fryer.
2. Then add Brussel sprouts, garlic powder, ground coriander, and apple cider vinegar.
3. Shake the vegetables gently and cook at 390F for 13 minutes. Shake the Brussel sprouts from time to time to avoid burning.

PER SERVING

Calories: 54 | Fat: 2.5g | Fiber: 2.9g | Carbs: 7.2g | Protein: 2.7g

Lemon Courgette Caviar

Prep Time: 5 minutes | Cook Time: 20 minutes | Serves 3

- 2 medium Courgettes
- 1 tablespoon olive oil
- 1 ½ tablespoons balsamic vinegar
- ½ red onion
- Juice of one lemon

1. Preheat your air fryer. Wash, then dry courgettes. Add lemon juice to over courgettes. Arrange courgettes in a baking dish, then bake them in the air fryer for 20-minutes.
2. Remove the courgettes from the oven and allow them to cool. Blend the onion in a blender. Slice the courgettes in half, lengthwise, then remove their insides using a spoon. Place courgettes into mixer and process everything. Add the vinegar, the olive oil and a little bit of salt, then blend again. Serve cool with tomato sauce.

PER SERVING

Calories: 76 | Total Fat: 0.3g | Carbs: 18g | Protein: 3g

Hot Pepper Pin Wheel

Prep Time: 3 minutes | Cook Time: 6 minutes | Serves 3

- 2 lbs. dill pickles
- 3 almond tortillas
- Salt and pepper to taste
- 3-ounces sliced ham
- 1 lb. softened cream
- 1 hot pepper, finely diced

1. Mix diced hot pepper in with cheese. On one side of the tortilla spread cheese over it. Place the ham slice over it. Spread a layer of cheese on top of ham slice. Roll 1 pickle up in the tortilla.
2. Preheat the air fryer to 340°Fahrenheit. Place the rolls in air fryer basket and cook for 6-minutes.

PER SERVING

Calories: 67 | Total Fat: 2.1g | Carbs: 0.11g | Protein: 3.2g

Cheese Zucchini Chips

Prep Time: 10 minutes | Cook Time: 13 minutes | Serves 8

- 2 zucchinis, thinly sliced
- 4 tablespoons almond flour
- 2 oz Parmesan
- 2 eggs, beaten
- ½ teaspoon white pepper
- Cooking spray

1. In the big bowl mix up almond flour, Parmesan, and white pepper. Then dip the zucchini slices in the egg and coat in the almond flour mixture.
2. Preheat the air fryer to 355F. Place the prepared zucchini slices in the air fryer in one layer and cook them for 10 minutes. Then flip the vegetables on another side and cook them for 3 minutes more or until crispy.

PER SERVING

Calories: 127 | Fat: 9.7g | Fiber: 2.1g | Carbs: 5.1g | Protein: 7.3g

Chocolate Bacon Bites

Prep Time: 5 minutes | Cook Time: 10 minutes | Serves 4

- 4 bacon slices, halved
- 1 cup dark chocolate, melted
- A pinch of pink salt

1. Dip each bacon slice in some chocolate, sprinkle pink salt over them, put them in your air fryer's basket and cook at 350 degrees F for 10 minutes.
2. Serve as a snack.

PER SERVING
Calories: 151 | Fat: 4g | Fiber: 2g | Carbs: 4g | Protein: 8g

Almond Coconut Granola

Prep Time: 10 minutes | Cook Time: 12 minutes | Serves 4

- 1 teaspoon monk fruit
- 1 teaspoon almond butter
- 1 teaspoon coconut oil
- 2 tablespoons almonds, chopped
- 1 teaspoon pumpkin puree
- ½ teaspoon pumpkin pie spices
- 2 tablespoons coconut flakes
- 2 tablespoons pumpkin seeds, crushed
- 1 teaspoon hemp seeds
- 1 teaspoon flax seeds
- Cooking spray

1. In the big bowl mix up almond butter and coconut oil. Microwave the mixture until it is melted. After this, in the separated bowl mix up monk fruit, pumpkin spices, coconut flakes, pumpkin seeds, hemp seeds, and flax seeds. Add the melted coconut oil and pumpkin puree. Then stir the mixture until it is homogenous.
2. Preheat the air fryer to 350F. Then put the pumpkin mixture on the baking paper and make the shape of the square. After this, cut the square on the serving bars and transfer in the preheated air fryer. Cook the pumpkin granola for 12 minutes.

PER SERVING
Calories: 91 | Fat: 8.2g | Fiber: 1.4g | Carbs: 3g | Protein: 3g

Deli Turkey and Avocado Roll-Ups
Prep Time: 5 minutes | Cook Time: 10 minutes | Serves 8

- 1/2 fresh lemon, juiced
- 2 avocados, pitted, peeled and diced
- 16 slices cooked turkey breasts, deli-sliced
- Salt and black pepper, to taste
- 16 slices Swiss cheese

1. Drizzle fresh lemon juice over your avocados. Place 1-2 avocado pieces on the turkey breast slice.
2. Season with salt and black pepper to taste.
3. Add the slice of Swiss cheese; repeat with the remaining ingredients. Roll them up and arrange on a nice serving platter. Bon appétit!

PER SERVING
Calories: 332 | Fat: 23.9g | Carbs: 7g | Protein: 22.4g | Fiber: 3.6g

Tomato Smokies
Prep Time: 15 minutes | Cook Time: 1045 minutes | Serves 10

- 12 oz pork and beef smokies
- 3 oz bacon, sliced
- 1 teaspoon keto tomato sauce
- 1 teaspoon Erythritol
- 1 teaspoon avocado oil
- ½ teaspoon cayenne pepper

1. Sprinkle the smokies with cayenne pepper and tomato sauce. Then sprinkle them with Erythritol and olive oil. After this, wrap every smokie in the bacon and secure it with the toothpick.
2. Preheat the air fryer to 400F. Place the bacon smokies in the air fryer and cook them for 10 minutes. Shake them gently during cooking to avoid burning.

PER SERVING
Calories: 126 | Fat: 9.7g | Fiber: 0.1g | Carbs: 1.4g | Protein: 8.7g

Pickled Bacon Bowls
Prep Time: 5 minutes | Cook Time: 20 minutes | Serves 4

- 4 dill pickle spears, sliced in half and quartered
- 8 bacon slices, halved
- 1 cup avocado mayonnaise

1. Wrap each pickle spear in a bacon slice, put them in your air fryer's basket and cook at 400 degrees F for 20 minutes.
2. Divide into bowls and serve as a snack with the mayonnaise.

PER SERVING
Calories: 100 | Fat: 4g | Fiber: 2g | Carbs: 3g | Protein: 4g

Turmeric Tempeh
Prep Time: 8 minutes | Cook Time: 12 minutes | Serves 4

- 1 teaspoon apple cider vinegar
- 1 tablespoon avocado oil
- ¼ teaspoon ground turmeric
- 6 oz tempeh, chopped

1. Mix avocado oil with apple cider vinegar and ground turmeric.
2. Then sprinkle the tempeh with turmeric mixture and put it in the air fryer basket.
3. Cook the tempeh at 350F for 12 minutes. Shake it after 6 minutes of cooking.

PER SERVING
Calories: 87 | Fat: 5g | Fiber: 0.2g | Carbs: 4.3g | Protein: 7.9g

Classic Hot Chicken Drumettes

Prep Time: 5 minutes | Cook Time: 25 minutes | Serves 6

- 2 pounds chicken drumettes
- Sea salt and ground black pepper, to taste
- 1/2 teaspoon paprika
- 1 teaspoon cayenne pepper
- 1 teaspoon dried oregano
- 1/3 cup hot sauce
- 1 tablespoon stone-ground mustard
- 1 teaspoon garlic powder

1. Pat dry the chicken drumettes with paper towels. Season them with salt, black pepper, paprika, cayenne pepper, and oregano.
2. Brush the drumettes with cooking oil and transfer to a roasting pan. Bake at 420 degrees F for 18 minutes.
3. Toss with the hot sauce, mustard and garlic powder; broil for 5 minutes more or until the chicken drumettes are golden brown and thoroughly cooked. Bon appétit!

PER SERVING
Calories: 179 | Fat: 2.5g | Carbs: 2.3g | Protein: 34.2g | Fiber: 0.7g

Coriander Fennel

Prep Time: 5 minutes | Cook Time: 15 minutes | Serves 4

- 1 pound fennel bulb, cut into small wedges
- 1 teaspoon ground coriander
- 1 tablespoon avocado oil
- ½ teaspoon salt

1. Rub the fennel bulb with ground coriander, avocado oil, and salt.
2. Put it in the air fryer basket and cook at 390F for 15 minutes. Flip the fennel on another side after 7 minutes of cooking.

PER SERVING
Calories: 40 | Fat: 0.7g | Fiber: 3.7g | Carbs: 8.5g | Protein: 1.2g

Banana Peppers Mix

Prep Time: 10 minutes | Cook Time: 20 minutes | Serves 4

- 8 oz banana peppers, chopped
- 1 tablespoon avocado oil
- 1 tablespoon dried oregano
- 2 tablespoons mascarpone
- 1 cup Monterey Jack cheese, shredded

1. Brush the baking pan with avocado oil.
2. After this, mix banana peppers with dried oregano and mascarpone and put in the prepared baking pan.
3. Top the peppers with Monterey Jack cheese and place in the air fryer basket.
4. Cook the meal at 365F for 20 minutes.

PER SERVING
Calories: 133 | Fat: 10.1g | Fiber: 1.1g | Carbs: 2.9g | Protein: 8.2g

Keto "Potato"

Prep Time: 10 minutes | Cook Time: 20 minutes | Serves 2

- 2 cups cauliflower, chopped
- 1 oz Parmesan, grated
- 1 tablespoon avocado oil

1. Sprinkle the cauliflower with avocado oil and put it in the air fryer.
2. Cook it at 390F for 10 minutes.
3. Then shake the cauliflower and sprinkle with Parmesan.
4. Cook the meal at 390F for 10 minutes more.

PER SERVING

Calories: 80 | Fat: 4g | Fiber: 2.8g | Carbs: 6.2g | Protein: 6.6g

Anchovies and Cheese Fat Bombs

Prep Time: 5 minutes | Cook Time: 0 minutes | Serves 2

- 2 (2-ounce) cans anchovies, drained
- 1/3 cup cream cheese, chilled
- 1/3 cup cheddar cheese, shredded
- 1 tablespoon Dijon mustard
- 2 scallions, chopped

1. Mix all of the above ingredients until everything is well incorporated. Shape the mixture into bite-sized balls.
2. Serve well chilled and enjoy!

PER SERVING

Calories: 391 | Fat: 26.6g | Carbs: 3.1g | Protein: 33.8g | Fiber: 0.7g

Cheesy Chicken and Ham Bites
Prep Time: 5 minutes | Cook Time: 25 minutes | Serves 5

- 5 slices ham
- 5 chicken fillets, about ¼-inch thin
- 3 ounces Ricotta cheese
- 1/3 cup Colby cheese, grated
- 1/2 cup spicy tomato sauce

1. Place a slice of ham on each chicken fillet.
2. Thoroughly combine the Ricotta cheese and Colby cheese until everything is well incorporated.
3. Then, divide the cheese mixture between the chicken fillets. Roll them up and secure with toothpicks.
4. Transfer them to a lightly oiled baking tray. Bake in the preheated oven at 390 degrees F for 18 minutes, flipping them once or twice.
5. Pour the spicy tomato sauce over the chicken roll-ups and bake another 4 to 6 minutes or until everything is thoroughly cooked. Bon appétit!

PER SERVING
Calories: 289 | Fat: 11.1g | Carbs: 7.2g | Protein: 36.8g | Fiber: 2g

Cocktail Meatballs with Cheese
Prep Time: 5 minutes | Cook Time: 25 minutes | Serves 10

- 1/2 ground turkey
- 1 pound ground beef
- 4 ounces pork rinds 1/4 cup full-fat milk
- 1 shallot, chopped
- 2 garlic cloves, minced
- Sea salt and ground black pepper, to taste
- 1/2 cup Romano cheese, grated

1. Thoroughly combine all ingredients in a mixing bowl; shape the mixture into bite-sized meatballs.
2. Place your meatballs on a parchment-lined baking sheet; brush your meatballs with olive oil.
3. Bake for 10 minutes; rotate the pan and bake for a further 10 minutes. Serve with cocktail sticks and enjoy!

PER SERVING
Calories: 247 | Fat: 18g | Carbs: 1.1g | Protein: 19.1g | Fiber: 0.1g

Chapter 6
Chicken and Poultry

Chicken Kebabs
Prep Time: 5 minutes | Cook Time: 15 minutes | Serves 3

- 1 lb. chicken breasts, diced
- 1 small zucchini, cut into rings
- 3 medium-sized bell peppers, sliced
- 2 medium tomatoes, sliced
- 6 large mushrooms, cut in halves
- ¼ cup sesame seeds
- ½ cup soy sauce
- 5 tablespoons honey
- 1 tablespoon olive oil
- Salt and pepper to taste
- Wooden skewers

1. Cut the chicken breasts into cubes and transfer to mixing bowl. Add salt and pepper. Add 1 tablespoon of olive oil and stir to blend. Add soy sauce and honey and sprinkle with sesame seeds. Set aside for 30-minutes. Alternately add chicken pieces and vegetables to wooden skewers.
2. Preheat your air fryer to 340°Fahrenheit. Place the chicken kebabs in fryer basket. Cook for 15-minutes.

PER SERVING
Calories: 289 | Total Fat: 11.2g | Carbs: 9.2g | Protein: 14.6g

Chicken Bites
Prep Time: 5 minutes | Cook Time: 15 minutes | Serves 4

- ¼ cup blue cheese salad dressing
- 1 lb. chicken breast, skinless and boneless
- ½ teaspoon salt
- 1 tablespoon olive oil
- ½ cup sour cream
- 1 cup breadcrumbs
- ¼ cup blue cheese, crumbled
- ½ teaspoon pepper

1. In a large bowl, mix the salad dressing, blue cheese, and sour cream. Stir and set aside. In another bowl, mix olive oil, salt, pepper, and breadcrumbs. Cut chicken breasts into 2-inch pieces and roll in breadcrumbs mixture.
2. Preheat air fryer to 380°Fahrenheit. Transfer the chicken bites to the frying basket. Cook for 15-minutes. Serve with sauce and enjoy!

PER SERVING
Calories: 290 | Total Fat: 11.3g | Carbs: 9.2g | Protein: 14.7g

Tandoori Chicken with Mint Yogurt
Prep Time: 5 minutes | Cook Time: 20 minutes | Serves 4

- 2-ounces of chicken breast
- 2 tablespoons tandoori paste, divided
- 4 tablespoons + ¾ cup Greek yogurt, divided
- 3 sprigs of mint, minced
- Salt and pepper to taste
- 1 tablespoon olive oil
- 2 cups cooked basmati rice
- Mint leaves for garnishing

1. Combine 1 tablespoon of tandoori paste and 2 tablespoons of yogurt in a bowl. Coat the chicken breast with mixture. Marinate for 2-hours in the fridge.
2. Preheat your air fryer to 360°Fahrenheit for 5-minutes. Set air fryer timer to 15-minutes and place the chicken inside. Prepare the mint yogurt sauce by mixing the minced mint with 2 tablespoons of yogurt. Season with salt and pepper and stir well. Prepare tandoori sauce: heat the olive oil in a pan over medium heat and sauté 1 tablespoon tandoori paste for 3-minutes. Add remaining ¾ cup of yogurt and sauté for another 2-minutes. Slice the chicken breast and serve with basmati rice. Cover meat with tandoori sauce and mint yogurt sauce on top. Garnish with mint leaves.

PER SERVING
Calories: 289 | Total Fat: 11.3g | Carbs: 9.7g | Protein: 14.8g

Coconut Chicken
Prep Time: 15 minutes | Cook Time: 12 minutes | Serves 4

- 12 oz chicken fillet (3 oz each fillet)
- 4 teaspoons coconut flakes
- 1 egg white, whisked
- 1 teaspoon salt
- ½ teaspoon ground black pepper
- Cooking spray

1. Beat the chicken fillets with the kitchen hammer and sprinkle with salt and ground black pepper. Then dip every chicken chop in the whisked egg white and coat in the coconut flakes.
2. Preheat the air fryer to 360F. Put the chicken chops in the air fryer and spray with cooking spray. Cook the chicken chop for 7 minutes. Then flip them on another side and cook for 5 minutes. The cooked chicken chops should have a golden brown color.

PER SERVING
Calories: 172 | Fat: 6.9g | Fiber: 0.2g | Carbs: 0.5g | Protein: 25.6g

Pesto Chicken
Prep Time: 10 minutes | Cook Time: 25 minutes | Serves 4

- 1 cup basil pesto
- 2 tablespoons olive oil
- A pinch of salt and black pepper
- 1 and ½ pounds chicken wings

1. In a bowl, mix the chicken wings with all the ingredients and toss well. Put the meat in the air fryer's basket and cook at 380 degrees F for 25 minutes. Divide between plates and serve.

PER SERVING
Calories: 244 | Fat: 11g | Fiber: 4g | Carbs: 6g | Protein: 17g

Hoisin Chicken
Prep Time: 25 minutes | Cook Time: 22 minutes | Serves 4

- ½ teaspoon hoisin sauce
- ½ teaspoon salt
- ½ teaspoon chili powder
- ½ teaspoon ground black pepper
- ½ teaspoon ground cumin
- ¼ teaspoon xanthan gum
- 1 teaspoon apple cider vinegar
- 1 tablespoon sesame oil
- 3 tablespoons coconut cream
- ½ teaspoon minced garlic
- ½ teaspoon chili paste
- 1-pound chicken drumsticks
- 2 tablespoons almond flour

1. Rub the chicken drumsticks with salt, chili powder, ground black pepper, ground cumin, and leave for 10 minutes to marinate. Meanwhile, in the mixing bowl mix up chili paste, minced garlic, coconut cream, apple cider vinegar, xanthan gum, and almond flour.
2. Coat the chicken drumsticks in the coconut cream mixture well, and leave to marinate for 10 minutes more.
3. Preheat the air fryer to 375F. Put the chicken drumsticks in the air fryer and cook them for 22 minutes.

PER SERVING
Calories: 279 | Fat: 14.5g | Fiber: 1.7g | Carbs: 3.4g | Protein: 32.4g

Turkey Crust Pizza with Bacon
Prep Time: 5 minutes | Cook Time: 32 minutes | Serves 4

- 1/2 pound ground turkey
- 1/2 cup Parmesan cheese, freshly grated
- 1/2 cup Mozzarella cheese, grated
- Salt and ground black pepper, to taste
- 1 bell pepper, sliced
- 2 slices Canadian bacon, chopped
- 1 tomato, chopped
- 1/2 teaspoon basil

1. In mixing bowl, thoroughly combine the ground turkey, cheese, salt, and black pepper.
2. Then, press the cheese-chicken mixture into a parchment-lined baking pan. Bake in the preheated oven, at 390 degrees F for 22 minutes.
3. Add bell pepper, bacon, tomato, oregano, and basil. Bake an additional 10 minutes and serve warm. Bon appétit!

PER SERVING
Calories: 360 | Fat: 22.7g | Carbs: 5.9g | Protein: 32.6g | Fiber: 0.7g

Chicken and Ghee Mix
Prep Time: 15 minutes | Cook Time: 30 minutes | Serves 4

- 12 oz chicken legs
- 1 teaspoon nutritional yeast
- 1 teaspoon chili flakes
- ½ teaspoon ground cumin
- 1 teaspoon ground turmeric
- ½ teaspoon ground paprika
- 1 teaspoon Splenda
- ¼ cup coconut flour
- 1 tablespoon ghee, melted

1. In the mixing bowl mix up nutritional yeast, chili flakes, ground cumin, garlic powder, ground turmeric, ground paprika, Splenda, and coconut flour. Then brush every chicken leg with ghee and coat well in the coconut flour mixture.
2. Preheat the air fryer to 380F. Place the chicken legs in the air fryer in one layer. Cook them for 15 minutes. Then flip the chicken legs on another side and cook them for 15 minutes more.

PER SERVING
Calories: 238 | Fat: 10.9g | Fiber: 3.5g | Carbs: 6.8g | Protein: 26.7g

Chicken Wrapped in Bacon
Prep Time: 5 minutes | Cook Time: 15 minutes | Serves 6

- 6 slices of bacon
- 1 small chicken breast
- 1 tablespoon garlic, minced
- Soft cheese

1. Chop up chicken breast into bite-sized pieces. Lay out bacon slices and spread cheese on top. Place chicken on top of cheese and roll up. Secure with a cocktail stick.
2. Place wrapped chicken pieces in air fryer and cooked for 15-minutes at 350°Fahrenheit.

PER SERVING
Calories: 296 | Total Fat: 11.8g | Carbs: 8.7g | Protein: 15.2g

Sun-dried Tomatoes and Chicken Mix
Prep Time: 5 minutes | Cook Time: 25 minutes | Serves 4

- 4 chicken thighs, skinless, boneless
- 1 tablespoon olive oil
- A pinch of salt and black pepper
- 1 tablespoon thyme, chopped
- 1 cup chicken stock
- 3 garlic cloves, minced
- ½ cup coconut cream
- 1 cup sun-dried tomatoes, chopped
- 4 tablespoons parmesan, grated

1. Heat up a pan that fits the air fryer with the oil over medium-high heat, add the chicken, salt, pepper and the garlic, and brown for 2-3 minutes on each side.
2. Add the rest of the ingredients except the parmesan, toss, put the pan in the air fryer and cook at 370 degrees F for 20 minutes. Sprinkle the parmesan on top, leave the mix aside for 5 minutes, divide everything between plates and serve.

PER SERVING
Calories: 275 | Fat: 12g | Fiber: 4g | Carbs: 6g | Protein: 17g

Chicken Quesadilla Melt
Prep Time: 15 minutes | Cook Time: 10 minutes | Serves 2

- 2 keto tortillas
- 9 oz chicken fillet, cooked, shredded
- 1 jalapeno pepper, sliced
- 3 oz Parmesan, grated
- 1 teaspoon dried dill

1. In the mixing bowl, mix shredded chicken with jalapeno pepper, Parmesan, and dried dill.
2. Then spread the mixture over the tortillas and fold them.
3. Put the tortillas in the air fryer basket and cook at 390F for 5 minutes per side.

PER SERVING
Calories: 532 | Fat: 26.6g | Fiber: 4.3g | Carbs: 10.2g | Protein: 62.8g

Special Chicken Salad
Prep Time: 20 minutes | Cook Time: 1 hour 20 minutes | Serves 3

- 1 chicken breast, skinless
- 1/4 mayonnaise
- 1/4 cup sour cream
- 2 tablespoons Cottage cheese, room temperature
- Salt and black pepper, to taste
- 1/4 cup sunflower seeds, hulled and roasted
- 1/2 avocado, peeled and cubed
- 1/2 teaspoon fresh garlic, minced
- 2 tablespoons scallions, chopped

1. Bring a pot of well-salted water to a rolling boil.
2. Add the chicken to the boiling water; now, turn off the heat, cover, and let the chicken stand in the hot water for 15 minutes.
3. Then, drain the water; chop the chicken into bite-sized pieces. Add the remaining ingredients and mix well.
4. Place in the refrigerator for at least one hour. Serve well chilled. Enjoy!

PER SERVING
Calories: 400 | Fat: 35.1g | Carbs: 5.6g | Protein: 16.1g | Fiber: 2.9g

Tangy Classic Chicken Drumettes
Prep Time: 10 minutes | Cook Time: 40 minutes | Serves 4

- 1 pound chicken drumettes
- 1 tablespoon olive oil
- 2 tablespoons butter, melted
- 1 garlic cloves, sliced
- Fresh juice of 1/2 lemon
- 2 tablespoons white wine
- Salt and ground black pepper, to taste
- 1 tablespoon fresh scallions, chopped

1. Start by preheating your oven to 440 degrees F. Place the chicken in a parchment-lined baking pan. Drizzle with olive oil and melted butter.
2. Add the garlic, lemon, wine, salt, and black pepper.
3. Bake in the preheated oven for about 35 minutes. Serve garnished with fresh scallions. Enjoy!

PER SERVING
Calories: 209 | Fat: 12.2g | Carbs: 0.4g | Protein: 23.2g | Fiber: 0.1g

Cumin Chicken Thighs
Prep Time: 5 minutes | Cook Time: 25 minutes | Serves 4

- 4 chicken thighs, skinless, boneless
- 1 tablespoon coconut oil
- 1 teaspoon ground cumin
- ½ teaspoon salt
- ½ teaspoon smoked paprika

1. Mix chicken thighs with coconut oil, cumin, salt, and smoked paprika.
2. Put the chicken thighs in the air fryer basket and cook at 375F for 25 minutes.

PER SERVING
Calories: 309 | Fat: 14.4g | Fiber: 0.2g | Carbs: 0.4g | Protein: 42.4g

Buttermilk Chicken

Prep Time: 5 minutes | Cook Time: 18 minutes | Serves 4

- 2 lbs. chicken thighs
- 2 teaspoons black pepper
- 1 teaspoon salt
- 1 tablespoon garlic powder
- 1 teaspoon cayenne pepper
- 1 tablespoon baking powder
- 2 cups almond flour
- 2 cups buttermilk
- 1 tablespoon paprika

1. Rinse the chicken thighs then pat dry. Add black pepper, paprika, and salt in a bowl. Toss the chicken pieces in paprika mixture. Pour buttermilk over chicken until coated. Place in the fridge for about 6-hours.
2. Preheat your air fryer to 355°Fahrenheit. Use a different bowl to mix flour, baking powder, salt, garlic powder and black pepper. Coat chicken thighs in seasoned flour. Remove any excess flour then place on a plate. Arrange the chicken in one layer on fryer basket and place basket inside air fryer and cook for 8-minutes.
3. Pull out the tray and turn chicken pieces over and cook for an additional 10-minutes.

PER SERVING

Calories: 292 | Total Fat: 11.3g | Carbs: 9.2g | Protein: 14.8g

Cream Cheese Chicken

Prep Time: 10 minutes | Cook Time: 25 minutes | Serves 5

- 1½-pound chicken breast, skinless, boneless
- 1 teaspoon ground paprika
- ½ teaspoon ground turmeric
- 2 teaspoons cream cheese
- 1 oz scallions, chopped
- 1 teaspoon avocado oil
- ½ teaspoon salt

1. Rub the chicken breast with ground paprika, turmeric, and salt.
2. Then put the chicken in the air fryer basket.
3. Add avocado oil, scallions, and cream cheese.
4. Cook the meal at 375F for 25 minutes.

PER SERVING

Calories: 165 | Fat: 4.1g | Fiber: 0.4g | Carbs: 0.9g | Protein: 29.1g

Ranch Chicken Breasts with Cheese

Prep Time: 5 minutes | Cook Time: 15 minutes | Serves 4

- 2 chicken breasts
- 2 tablespoons butter, melted
- 1 teaspoon salt
- 1/2 teaspoon garlic powder
- 1/2 teaspoon cayenne pepper
- 1/2 teaspoon black peppercorns, crushed
- 1/2 tablespoon ranch seasoning mix
- 4 ounces Ricotta cheese, room temperature
- 1/2 cup Monterey-Jack cheese, grated
- 4 slices bacon, chopped
- 1/4 cup scallions, chopped

1. Start by preheating your oven to 370 degrees F.
2. Drizzle the chicken with melted butter. Rub the chicken with salt, garlic powder, cayenne pepper, black pepper, and ranch seasoning mix.
3. Heat a cast iron skillet over medium heat. Cook the chicken for 3 to 5 minutes per side. Transfer the chicken to a lightly greased baking dish.
4. Add cheese and bacon. Bake about 12 minutes. Top with scallions just before serving. Bon appétit!

PER SERVING

Calories: 295 | Fat: 19.5g | Carbs: 2.9g | Protein: 25.5g | Fiber: 0g

Jalapeno Chicken Drumsticks

Prep Time: 5 minutes | Cook Time: 25 minutes | Serves 4

- 2-pound chicken drumsticks
- 2 jalapeno peppers, minced
- 1 tablespoon avocado oil
- 1 teaspoon ground black pepper
- ½ teaspoon garlic powder

1. In the mixing bowl mix chicken drumsticks with jalapeno peppers, avocado oil, ground black pepper, and garlic powder.
2. Put the chicken drumsticks in the air fryer and cook at 370F for 25 minutes.

PER SERVING

Calories: 393 | Fat: 13.5g | Fiber: 0.6g | Carbs: 1.3g | Protein: 62.6g

Chicken and Olives Mix

Prep Time: 10 minutes | Cook Time: 30 minutes | Serves 4

- 8 chicken thighs, boneless and skinless
- A pinch of salt and black pepper
- 2 tablespoons olive oil
- 1 teaspoon oregano, dried
- ½ teaspoon garlic powder
- 1 cup pepperoncini, drained and sliced
- ½ cup black olives, pitted and sliced
- ½ cup kalamata olives, pitted and sliced
- ¼ cup parmesan, grated

1. Heat up a pan that fits the air fryer with the oil over medium-high heat, add the chicken and brown for 2 minutes on each side. Add salt, pepper, and all the other ingredients except the parmesan and toss.
2. Put the pan in the air fryer, sprinkle the parmesan on top and cook at 370 degrees F for 25 minutes. Divide the chicken mix between plates and serve.

PER SERVING

Calories: 270 | Fat: 14g | Fiber: 4g | Carbs: 6g | Protein: 18g

Provolone Chicken Breasts

Prep Time: 5 minutes | Cook Time: 24 minutes | Serves 6

- 3-pounds chicken breast, skinless, boneless
- 1 tablespoon coconut oil
- 5 oz provolone cheese, shredded
- 1 teaspoon dried oregano
- 1 teaspoon dried cilantro

1. Rub the chicken breast with dried oregano and cilantro.
2. Then brush the chicken breast with coconut oil and put it in the air fryer basket.
3. Cook it for 20 minutes at 385F.
4. Then top the chicken breast with Provolone cheese and cook the meal for 4 minutes more.

PER SERVING

Calories: 362 | Fat: 14.3g | Fiber: 0.1g | Carbs: 0.7g | Protein: 54.2g

Easy Turkey Curry

Prep Time: 10 minutes | Cook Time: 1 hour | Serves 4

- 3 teaspoons sesame oil
- 1 pound turkey wings, boneless and chopped
- 2 cloves garlic, finely chopped
- 1 small-sized red chili pepper, minced
- 1/2 teaspoon turmeric powder
- 1/2 teaspoon ginger powder
- 1 teaspoon red curry paste
- 1 cup unsweetened coconut milk, preferably homemade
- 1/2 cup water
- 1/2 cup turkey consommé
- Kosher salt and ground black pepper, to taste

1. Heat sesame oil in a sauté pan. Add the turkey and cook until it is light brown about 7 minutes.
2. Add garlic, chili pepper, turmeric powder, ginger powder, and curry paste and cook for 3 minutes longer.
3. Add the milk, water, and consommé. Season with salt and black pepper. Cook for 45 minutes over medium heat. Bon appétit!

PER SERVING

Calories: 295 | Fat: 19.5g | Carbs: 2.9g | Protein: 25.5g | Fiber: 0g

Cheesy Chicken Drumsticks

Prep Time: 5 minutes | Cook Time: 15 minutes | Serves 2

- 1 tablespoon peanut oil
- 2 chicken drumsticks
- 1/2 cup vegetable broth
- 1/2 cup cream cheese
- 2 cups baby spinach
- Sea salt and ground black pepper, to taste
- 1/2 teaspoon parsley flakes
- 1/2 teaspoon shallot powder
- 1/2 teaspoon garlic powder
- 1/2 cup Asiago cheese, grated

1. Heat the oil in a pan over medium-high heat. Then cook the chicken for 7 minutes, turning occasionally; reserve.
2. Pour in broth; add cream cheese and spinach; cook until spinach has wilted. Add the chicken back to the pan.
3. Add seasonings and Asiago cheese; cook until everything is thoroughly heated, an additional 4 minutes. Serve immediately and enjoy!

PER SERVING

Calories: 589 | Fat: 46g | Carbs: 5.8g | Protein: 37.5g | Fiber: 1g

Chapter 7
Beef, Lamb and Pork

Air-Fried Roast Beef

Prep Time: 10 minutes | Cook Time: 55 minutes | Serves 6

- 2 lbs. round roast
- ½ teaspoon garlic powder
- ½ teaspoon oregano
- 1 teaspoon dried thyme
- 1 tablespoon olive oil
- 1 teaspoon onion powder
- Salt and black pepper to taste

1. Preheat the air fryer to 330°Fahrenheit. Mix all the spices in a small bowl. Brush the olive oil on the beef. Rub the spice mixture into the beef. Place in baking dish in air fryer for 30-minutes, then flip and cook for another 25-minutes.
2. Serve warm.

PER SERVING

Calories: 304 | Total Fat: 12.8g | Carbs: 11.7g | Protein: 16.8g

Air Fryer Classic Beef Pot Roast

Prep Time: 10 minutes | Cook Time: 60 minutes | Serves 4

- 1 lb. chuck roast
- 4 spring onions
- 2 cinnamon sticks
- 2 tablespoons of ginger garlic paste
- 2 tablespoons of olive oil
- 1 teaspoon paprika
- 2 cardamoms
- 1 cup of water
- ½ cup of fresh coriander, chopped
- Salt and pepper to taste
- 1 bay leaf

1. Preheat your air fryer to 400°Fahrenheit. Cut the chuck roast into medium-sized chunks. In a large bowl, add beef, onion, ginger garlic paste, salt, pepper, bay leaf, coriander, cardamoms, paprika, and water. Mix well and marinate for 1-hour.
2. Add everything to casserole dish and roast in the air fryer for 1-hour. Remove bay leaf then serve hot!

PER SERVING

Calories: 303 | Total Fat: 12.6g | Carbs: 11.3g | Protein: 16.4g

Tasty Beef Burgers

Prep Time: 5 minutes | Cook Time: 18 minutes | Serves 4

- 1 ½ lbs. ground beef
- 1 tablespoon Montreal steak seasoning
- 1 cup cheddar cheese, shredded
- 1 tablespoon Worcestershire sauce
- ½ cup cheese sauce

1. Preheat your air fryer to 370°Fahrenheit. Add the ground beef, Montreal steak seasoning, Worcestershire sauce in a bowl and mix well. Make four patties from mixture and place in preheated air fryer basket and cook for 15-minutes.
2. Flip the patties halfway through. Combine the cheese sauce and cheddar cheese. Add cheese mixture to the top of patties and cook for an additional 3-minutes. Serve warm!

PER SERVING

Calories: 302 | Total Fat: 12.3g | Carbs: 11.2g | Protein: 16.4g

Onion Carrot Meatloaf

Prep Time: 5 minutes | Cook Time: 25 minutes | Serves 6

- 1 lb. ground beef
- Salt and pepper to taste
- ½ cup breadcrumbs
- ¼ cup milk
- ½ onion, shredded
- 2 carrots, shredded
- 1 egg

1. Preheat your air fryer to 400°Fahrenheit. Mix all your ingredients in a bowl.
2. Add the meatloaf mixture to a loaf pan and place it in your air fryer basket. Cook in air fryer for 25-minutes and serve warm.

PER SERVING

Calories: 306 | Total Fat: 12.7g | Carbs: 12.3g | Protein: 16.8g

Pork with Peppercorn Tomato Sauce
Prep Time: 5 minutes | Cook Time: 25 minutes | Serves 4

- 1 tablespoon mustard
- ¼ cup keto tomato sauce
- 4 pork chops
- A pinch of salt and black pepper
- 1 teaspoon garlic powder
- 2 teaspoons smoked paprika
- 1 and ½ teaspoons peppercorns, crushed
- A pinch of cayenne pepper
- A drizzle of olive oil

1. Heat up a pan that fits your air fryer with the oil over medium heat, add the pork chops and brown for 5 minutes. Add the rest of the ingredients, toss, put the pan in the fryer and cook at 400 degrees F for 20 minutes.
2. Divide everything between plates and serve.

PER SERVING
Calories: 280 | Fat: 13g | Fiber: 4g | Carbs: 6g | Protein: 18g

Spiced Chops
Prep Time: 10 minutes | Cook Time: 12 minutes | Serves 3

- 10 oz pork chops, bone-in (3 pork chops)
- 1 teaspoon Erythritol
- 1 teaspoon ground black pepper
- 1 teaspoon ground paprika
- ½ teaspoon onion powder
- ¼ teaspoon garlic powder
- 2 teaspoons olive oil

1. In the mixing bowl mix up Erythritol, ground black pepper, ground paprika, onion powder, and garlic powder. Then rub the pork chops with the spice mixture from both sides. After this, sprinkle the meat with olive oil. Leave the meat for 5-10 minutes to marinate.
2. Preheat the air fryer to 400F. Put the pork chops in the air fryer and cook them for 6 minutes. Then flip the meat on another side and cook it for 6 minutes more.

PER SERVING
Calories: 335 | Fat: 26.7g | Fiber: 0.5g | Carbs: 1.3g | Protein: 21.5g

Lemon Pork
Prep Time: 15 minutes | Cook Time: 25 minutes | Serves 4

- 4 pork chops
- 2 tablespoons olive oil
- A pinch of salt and black pepper
- 2 garlic cloves, minced
- 4 teaspoons mustard
- 2 teaspoons lemon zest, grated
- Juice of 1 lemon

1. In a bowl, mix the pork chops with the other ingredients, toss and keep in the fridge for 15 minutes Put the pork chops in your air fryer's basket and cook at 390 degrees F for 25 minutes.
2. Divide between plates and serve with a side salad.

PER SERVING
Calories: 287 | Fat: 13g | Fiber: 4g | Carbs: 6g | Protein: 20g

Pork Cutlets with Spanish Onion
Prep Time: 5 minutes | Cook Time: 15 minutes | Serves 2

- 1 tablespoon olive oil
- 2 pork cutlets
- 1 bell pepper, deveined and sliced
- 1 Spanish onion, chopped
- 2 garlic cloves, minced
- 1/2 teaspoon hot sauce
- 1/2 teaspoon mustard
- 1/2 teaspoon paprika
- Coarse sea salt and ground black pepper, to taste

1. Heat the olive oil in a large saucepan over medium-high heat.
2. Then, fry the pork cutlets for 3 to 4 minutes until evenly golden and crispy on both sides.
3. Decrease the temperature to medium and add the bell pepper, Spanish onion, garlic, hot sauce, and mustard; continue cooking until the vegetables have softened, for a further 3 minutes.
4. Sprinkle with paprika, salt, and black pepper. Serve immediately and enjoy!

PER SERVING
Calories: 403 | Fat: 24.1g | Carbs: 3.4g | Total Carbs: 40.1g | Fiber: 0.7g

Thyme and Turmeric Pork

Prep Time: 10 minutes | Cook Time: 15 minutes | Serves 4

- pound pork tenderloin
- ½ teaspoon salt
- ½ teaspoon ground turmeric
- 1 tablespoon dried thyme
- 1 tablespoon avocado oil

1. Rub the pork tenderloin with salt, ground turmeric, and dried thyme. Then brush it with avocado oil.
2. Preheat the air fryer to 370F. Place the pork tenderloin in the air fryer basket and cook it for 15 minutes. You can flip the meat on another side during cooking if desired.

PER SERVING

Calories: 170 | Fat: 4.5g | Fiber: 0.5g | Carbs: 0.8g | Protein: 29.8g

Parmesan Meatballs

Prep Time: 15 minutes | Cook Time: 8 minutes | Serves 6

- 10 oz ground beef
- 4 oz ground pork
- 1 tablespoon taco seasoning
- 1 oz Parmesan, grated
- 1 teaspoon dried cilantro
- 1 teaspoon sesame oil

1. In the mixing bowl mix up ground beef, ground pork, taco seasonings, and dried cilantro. When the mixture is homogenous, add Parmesan cheese and stir it well. With the help of the scooper make the medium-size meatballs.
2. Preheat the air fryer to 385F. Brush the air fryer basket with sesame oil from inside and put the meatballs. Arrange them in one layer. Cook the meatballs for 8 minutes. Flip them on another side after 4 minutes of cooking.

PER SERVING

Calories: 142 | Fat: 5.4g | Fiber: 0g | Carbs: 1.2g | Protein: 20.8g

Sweet & Tangy Meatballs

Prep Time: 5 minutes | Cook Time: 15 minutes | Serves 24

- 1 lb. ground beef
- 1 tablespoon liquid stevia
- ½ teaspoon dry mustard
- ½ teaspoon ginger, ground
- ¾ cup tomato ketchup
- 1 tablespoon Tabasco sauce
- 1 tablespoon Worcestershire sauce
- ¼ cup vinegar
- 1 tablespoon lemon juice

1. In a bowl, combine all the ingredients. Make small meatballs from the mixture and place them in air fryer basket. Air fry meatballs at 370°Fahrenheit for 15-minutes. Serve warm.

PER SERVING

Calories: 298 | Total Fat: 12.2g | Carbs: 11.6g | Protein: 15.8g

Tender Pork

Prep Time: 20 minutes | Cook Time: 40 minutes | Serves 5

- 3-pound pork shoulder
- 1 tablespoon cream cheese
- 1 tablespoon avocado oil
- 1 tablespoon lemon juice
- ½ teaspoon salt
- ½ tablespoon cayenne pepper

1. In the shallow bowl mix cream cheese with avocado oil, lemon juice, salt, and cayenne pepper.
2. Carefully rub the pork shoulder with cream cheese mixture and leave for 15 minutes to marinate.
3. Then sprinkle the pork shoulder with avocado oil and put it in the air fryer.
4. Cook the pork at 360F for 40 minutes.

PER SERVING

Calories: 808 | Fat: 59.4g | Fiber: 0.3g | Carbs: 0.6g | Protein: 63.6g

Melt-in-Your-Mouth Pork Roast

Prep Time: 15 minutes plus marinating time | Cook Time: 1 hour | Serves 2

- 1 pound pork shoulder
- 4 tablespoons red wine
- 1 teaspoon stone ground mustard
- 1 tablespoon coconut aminos
- 1 tablespoon lemon juice
- 1 tablespoon sesame oil
- 2 sprigs rosemary
- 1 teaspoon sage
- 1 shallot, peeled and chopped
- 1/2 celery stalk, chopped
- 1/2 head garlic, peeled and separated into cloves
- Sea salt and freshly cracked black pepper, to season

1. Place the pork shoulder, red wine, mustard, coconut aminos, lemon juice, sesame oil, rosemary, and sage in a ceramic dish; cover and let it marinate in your refrigerator at least 3 hours.
2. Discard the marinade and place the pork shoulder in a lightly greased baking dish. Scatter the vegetables around the pork shoulder and sprinkle with salt and black pepper.
3. Roast in the preheated oven at 390 degrees F for 15 minutes.
4. Now, reduce the temperature to 310 degrees F and continue baking an additional 40 to 45 minutes. Baste the meat with the reserved marinade once or twice.
5. Place on cooling racks before carving and serving. Bon appétit!

PER SERVING
Calories: 497 | Fat: 35.3g | Carbs: 2.5g | Total Carbs: 40.2g | Fiber: 0.6g

Vinegar Pork Chops

Prep Time: 10 minutes | Cook Time: 20 minutes | Serves 4

- 4 pork chops
- ¼ cup apple cider vinegar
- 1 teaspoon ground black pepper
- 1 teaspoon olive oil

1. Mix apple cider vinegar with olive oil and ground black pepper.
2. Then mix pork chops with apple cider vinegar mixture.
3. Put the meat in the air fryer and cook it at 375F for 10 minutes per side.

PER SERVING
Calories: 271 | Fat: 21.1g | Fiber: 0.1g | Carbs: 0.5g | Protein: 18g

African Style Pork Shoulder

Prep Time: 25 minutes | Cook Time: 50 minutes | Serves 4

- 2-pound pork shoulder
- 1 teaspoon dried sage
- 1 teaspoon curry powder
- ¼ cup plain yogurt
- 1 tablespoon avocado oil

1. Mix curry powder with plain yogurt and avocado oil.
2. Add dried sage and stir the mixture.
3. Then brush the pork shoulder with plain yogurt mixture and leave for 20 minutes to marinate.
4. Then transfer the pork shoulder in the air fryer. Add all remaining yogurt mixture.
5. Cook the meal at 365F for 50 minutes.

PER SERVING
Calories: 680 | Fat: 49.2g | Fiber: 0.4g | Carbs: 1.7g | Protein: 53.8g

Pork Stuffing

Prep Time: 10 minutes | Cook Time: 35 minutes | Serves 6

- 4 oz pork rinds
- 2 pecans, chopped
- 1 teaspoon Italian seasonings
- ½ teaspoon white pepper
- 1 egg, beaten
- 4 tablespoons almond flour
- 3 cups ground pork
- 1 tablespoon avocado oil
- ¼ cup heavy cream

1. Put all ingredients in the mixing bowl and stir until homogenous.
2. Then transfer the mixture in the air fryer and cook it at 360F for 35 minutes.
3. Stir the meal every 10 minutes.

PER SERVING
Calories: 667 | Fat: 47.9g | Fiber: 1.2g | Carbs: 2.2g | Protein: 54.9g

Dijon Pork Chops

Prep Time: 10 minutes | Cook Time: 20 minutes | Serves 4

- 4 pork chops
- 1 tablespoon Dijon mustard
- 1 teaspoon chili powder
- 1 tablespoon avocado oil

1. Mix Dijon mustard with chili powder and avocado oil.
2. Then carefully brush the pork chops with the mustard mixture from both sides.
3. Cook the pork chops at 375F for 10 minutes per side.

PER SERVING

Calories: 265 | Fat: 20.6g | Fiber: 0.5g | Carbs: 0.8g | Protein: 18.3g

Rich and Easy Pork Ragout

Prep Time: 10 minutes | Cook Time: 40 minutes | Serves 2

- 1 teaspoon lard, melted at room temperature
- 3/4 pound pork butt, cut into bite-sized cubes
- 1 red bell pepper, deveined and chopped
- 1 poblano pepper, deveined and chopped
- 2 cloves garlic, pressed
- 1/2 cup leeks, chopped
- Sea salt and ground black pepper, to season
- 1/2 teaspoon mustard seeds
- 1/4 teaspoon ground allspice
- 1/4 teaspoon celery seeds
- 1 cup roasted vegetable broth
- 2 vine-ripe tomatoes, pureed

1. Melt the lard in a stockpot over moderate heat. Once hot, cook the pork cubes for 4 to 6 minutes, stirring occasionally to ensure even cooking.
2. Then, stir in the vegetables and continue cooking until they are tender and fragrant. Add in the salt, black pepper, mustard seeds, allspice, celery seeds, roasted vegetable broth, and tomatoes.
3. Reduce the heat to simmer. Let it simmer for 30 minutes longer or until everything is heated through.
4. Ladle into individual bowls and serve hot. Bon appétit!

PER SERVING

Calories: 389 | Fat: 24.3g | Carbs: 5.4g | Total Carbs: 33.1g | Fiber: 1.3g

Chunky Pork Soup with Mustard Greens

Prep Time: 5 minutes | Cook Time: 25 minutes | Serves 2

- 1 tablespoon olive oil
- 1 bell pepper, deveined and chopped
- 2 garlic cloves, pressed
- 1/2 cup scallions, chopped
- 1/2 pound ground pork (84% lean)
- 1 cup beef bone broth
- 1 cup water
- 1/2 teaspoon crushed red pepper flakes
- Sea salt and freshly cracked black pepper, to season
- 1 bay laurel
- 1 teaspoon fish sauce
- 2 cups mustard greens, torn into pieces
- 1 tablespoon fresh parsley, chopped

1. Heat the olive oil in a stockpot over a moderate flame. Coat, once hot, sauté the pepper, garlic, and scallions until tender or about 3 minutes.
2. After that, stir in the ground pork and cook for 5 minutes more or until well browned, stirring periodically.
3. Add in the beef bone broth, water, red pepper, salt, black pepper, and bay laurel. Reduce the temperature to simmer and cook, covered, for 10 minutes. Afterwards, stir in the fish sauce and mustard greens.
4. Remove from the heat; let it stand until the greens are wilted. Ladle into individual bowls and serve garnished with fresh parsley.

PER SERVING

Calories: 344 | Fat: 25.2g | Carbs: 6.3g | Total Carbs: 23.1g | Fiber: 2.9g

The Ultimate UK Keto Diet for Beginners

Chapter 8
Fish and Seafood

Salmon with Dill Sauce

Prep Time: 5 minutes | **Cook Time:** 23 minutes | **Serves 4**

- 1 ½ lbs. of salmon
- 4 teaspoons olive oil
- Pinch of sea salt
- ½ cup non-fat Greek yogurt
- ½ cup light sour cream
- 2 tablespoons dill, finely chopped
- Pinch of sea salt

1. Preheat your air fryer to 270°Fahrenheit. Cut salmon into four 6-ounce portions and drizzle 1 teaspoon of olive oil over each piece. Season with sea salt. Place salmon into cooking basket and cook for 23-minutes.
2. Make dill sauce. In a mixing bowl, mix sour cream, yogurt, chopped dill and sea salt. Top cooked salmon with sauce and garnish with additional dill and serve.

PER SERVING

Calories: 303 | Total Fat: 10.2g | Carbs: 8.9g | Protein: 14.8gg

Air-Fried Asian Style Fish

Prep Time: 5 minutes | **Cook Time:** 20 minutes | **Serves 2**

- 1 medium sea bass
- or halibut (12-ounces)
- 2 garlic cloves, minced
- 1 tablespoon olive oil
- 3 slices of ginger, julienned
- 2 tablespoons cooking wine
- 1 tomato, cut into quarters
- 1 lime, thinly cut
- 1 green onion, chopped
- 1 chili, diced

1. Prepare ginger, garlic oil mixture: sauté ginger and garlic with oil until golden brown in a small saucepan over medium-heat on top of the stove. Preheat your air fryer to 360°Fahrenheit.
2. Prepare fish: clean, rinse, and pat dry. Cut in half to fit into air fryer. Place the fish inside of air fryer basket then drizzle it with cooking wine. Layer tomato and lime slices on top of fish. Cover with garlic ginger oil mixture. Top with green onion and slices of chili. Cover with aluminum foil. Cook for 20-minutes.

PER SERVING

Calories: 304 | Total Fat: 9.2g | Carbs: 8.2g | Protein: 16.2g

Chili Haddock

Prep Time: 10 minutes | **Cook Time:** 8 minutes | **Serves 4**

- 12 oz haddock fillet
- 1 egg, beaten
- 1 teaspoon cream cheese
- 1 teaspoon chili flakes
- ½ teaspoon salt
- Cooking spray

1. Cut the haddock on 4 pieces and sprinkle with chili flakes and salt. After this, in the small bowl mix up egg and cream cheese. Dip the haddock pieces in the egg mixture and generously sprinkle with flax meal.
2. Preheat the air fryer to 400F. Put the prepared haddock pieces in the air fryer in one layer and cook them for 4 minutes from each side or until they are golden brown.

PER SERVING

Calories: 122 | Fat: 2.8g | Fiber: 0.5g | Carbs: 0.6g | Protein: 22.5g

Lime Cod

Prep Time: 5 minutes | **Cook Time:** 14 minutes | **Serves 4**

- 4 cod fillets, boneless
- 1 tablespoon olive oil
- 2 teaspoons sweet paprika
- Juice of 1 lime

1. In a bowl, mix all the ingredients, transfer the fish to your air fryer's basket and cook 350 degrees F for 7 minutes on each side. Divide the fish between plates and serve with a side salad.

PER SERVING

Calories: 240 | Fat: 14g | Fiber: 2g | Carbs: 4g | Protein: 16g

Blackened Salmon

Prep Time: 10 minutes | **Cook Time:** 8 minutes | **Serves 2**

- 10 oz salmon fillet
- ½ teaspoon ground coriander
- 1 teaspoon ground cumin
- 1 teaspoon dried basil
- 1 tablespoon avocado oil

1. In the shallow bowl, mix ground coriander, ground cumin, and dried basil.
2. Then coat the salmon fillet in the spices and sprinkle with avocado oil.
3. Put the fish in the air fryer basket and cook at 395F for 4 minutes per side.

PER SERVING

Calories: 201 | Fat: 9.9g | Fiber: 0.4g | Carbs: 0.9g | Protein: 27.8g

Tilapia and Kale
Prep Time: 5 minutes | Cook Time: 20 minutes | Serves 4

- 4 tilapia fillets, boneless
- Salt and black pepper to the taste
- 2 garlic cloves, minced
- 1 teaspoon fennel seeds
- ½ teaspoon red pepper flakes, crushed
- 1 bunch kale, chopped
- 3 tablespoons olive oil

1. In a pan that fits the fryer, combine all the ingredients, put the pan in the fryer and cook at 360 degrees F for 20 minutes. Divide everything between plates and serve.

PER SERVING
Calories: 240 | Fat: 12g | Fiber: 2g | Carbs: 4g | Protein: 12g

Mackerel with Spring Onions and Peppers
Prep Time: 15 minutes | Cook Time: 20 minutes | Serves 5

- pound mackerel, trimmed
- 1 tablespoon ground paprika
- 1 green bell pepper
- ½ cup spring onions, chopped
- 1 tablespoon avocado oil
- 1 teaspoon apple cider vinegar
- ½ teaspoon salt

1. Wash the mackerel if needed and sprinkle with ground paprika. Chop the green bell pepper. Then fill the mackerel with bell pepper and spring onion. After this, sprinkle the fish with avocado oil, apple cider vinegar, and salt.
2. Preheat the air fryer to 375F. Place the mackerel in the air fryer basket and cook it for 20 minutes.

PER SERVING
Calories: 258 | Fat: 16.8g | Fiber: 1.2g | Carbs: 3.8g | Protein: 22.2g

Black Cod with Grapes, Pecans, Fennel & Kale
Prep Time: 5 minutes | Cook Time: 15 minutes | Serves 2

- 2 fillets black cod (8-ounces)
- 3 cups kale, minced
- 2 teaspoons white balsamic vinegar
- ½ cup pecans
- 1 cup grapes, halved
- 1 small bulb fennel, cut into inch-thick slices
- 4 tablespoons extra-virgin olive oil
- Salt and black pepper to taste

1. Preheat your air fryer to 400°Fahrenheit. Use salt and pepper to season your fish fillets. Drizzle with 1 teaspoon of olive oil. Place the fish inside of air fryer with the skin side down and cook for 10-minutes.
2. Take the fish out and cover loosely with aluminum foil. Combine fennel, pecans, and grapes. Pour 2 tablespoons of olive oil and season with salt and pepper. Add to the air fryer basket. Cook for an additional 5-minutes.
3. In a bowl combine minced kale and cooked grapes, fennel and pecans. Cover ingredients with balsamic vinegar and remaining 1 tablespoon of olive oil. Toss gently. Serve fish with sauce and enjoy!

PER SERVING
Calories: 289 | Total Fat: 9.2g | Carbs: 8.6g | Protein: 16.3g

Grilled Salmon with Capers & Dill
Prep Time: 3 minutes | Cook Time: 8 minutes | Serves 2

- 1 teaspoon capers, chopped
- 2 sprigs dill, chopped
- 1 lemon zest
- 1 tablespoon olive oil
- 4 slices lemon (optional)
- 11-ounce salmon fillet
- 5 capers, chopped
- 1 sprig dill, chopped
- 2 tablespoons plain yogurt
- Pinch of lemon zest
- Salt and black pepper to taste

1. Preheat your air fryer to 400°Fahrenheit. Mix dill, capers, lemon zest, olive oil and salt in a bowl. Cover the salmon with this mixture. Cook salmon for 8-minutes.
2. Combine the dressing ingredients in another bowl. When salmon is cooked, place on serving plate and drizzle dressing over it. Place lemon slices at the side of the plate and serve.

PER SERVING
Calories: 300 | Total Fat: 8.9g | Carbs: 7.3g | Protein: 16.2g

Cumin Catfish
Prep Time: 5 minutes | Cook Time: 15 minutes | Serves 4

- 1 tablespoon ground cumin
- 1 tablespoon avocado oil
- ½ teaspoon apple cider vinegar
- 1-pound catfish fillet

1. Rub the catfish fillet with ground cumin, avocado oil, and apple cider vinegar/
2. Put the fish in the air fryer and cook at 360F for 15 minutes.

PER SERVING
Calories: 164 | Fat: 9.4g | Fiber: 0.3g | Carbs: 0.9g | Protein: 17.9g

Tender Tilapia
Prep Time: 5 minutes | Cook Time: 20 minutes | Serves 4

- 4 tilapia fillets, boneless
- 1 tablespoon ghee
- 1 tablespoon apple cider vinegar
- 1 teaspoon dried cilantro

1. Sprinkle the tilapia fillets with apple cider vinegar and dried cilantro.
2. Put the fish in the air fryer basket, add ghee, and cook it at 375F for 10 minutes per side.

PER SERVING
Calories: 122 | Fat: 4.2g | Fiber: 0g | Carbs: 0g | Protein: 21g

Rosemary Shrimp Skewers
Prep Time: 10 minutes | Cook Time: 5 minutes | Serves 5

- 4-pounds shrimps, peeled
- 1 tablespoon dried rosemary
- 1 tablespoon avocado oil
- 1 teaspoon apple cider vinegar

1. Mix the shrimps with dried rosemary, avocado oil, and apple cider vinegar.
2. Then sting the shrimps into skewers and put in the air fryer.
3. Cook the shrimps at 400F for 5 minutes.

PER SERVING
Calories: 437 | Fat: 6.6g | Fiber: 0.4g | Carbs: 6.1g | Protein: 82.7g

Pan Fried Garlicky Fish
Prep Time: 5 minutes | Cook Time: 15 minutes | Serves 2

- 1 tablespoon olive oil
- 2 mackerel fillets
- 2 garlic cloves, minced
- Sea salt and ground black pepper, to taste
- 1/2 teaspoon thyme
- 1 teaspoon rosemary
- 1/2 teaspoon basil

1. Heat the olive oil in a frying pan over a moderate flame and swirl to coat the bottom of the pan. Pat dry the mackerel fillets.
2. Now, brown the fish fillets for 5 minutes per side until golden and crisp, shaking the pan lightly.
3. During the last minutes, add the garlic, salt, black pepper, and herbs. Bon appétit!

PER SERVING
Calories: 481 | Fat: 14.5g | Carbs: 1.1g | Protein: 80g | Fiber: 0.1g

Chapter 9
Vegetarian Recipes

Coconut Chips

Prep Time: 3 minutes | Cook Time: 5 minutes | Serves 2

- 2 cups large pieces of shredded coconut
- 1/3 teaspoon liquid Stevia
- 1 tablespoon chili powder

1. Preheat your air fryer to 390°Fahrenheit. Combine the shredded coconut pieces with spices. Cook for 5-minutes in air fryer and enjoy!

PER SERVING
Calories: 261 | Total Fat: 9.2g | Carbs: 7.3g | Protein: 6.2g

Sweet Potato Chips

Prep Time: 5 minutes | Cook Time: 15 minutes | Serves 2

- 2 large sweet potatoes, thinly sliced with Mandoline
- 2 tablespoons olive oil
- Salt to taste

1. Preheat your air fryer to 350°Fahrenheit. Stir the sweet potato slices, in a large bowl with the oil. Arrange slices in your air fryer and cook them until crispy, for about 15-minutes.

PER SERVING
Calories: 253 | Total Fat: 11.2g | Carbs: 8.4g | Protein: 6.5g

Vegetable Spring Rolls

Prep Time: 5 minutes | Cook Time: 23 minutes | Serves 10

- 10 spring roll wrappers
- 2 tablespoons cornstarch
- Water
- 3 green onions, thinly sliced
- 1 tablespoon black pepper
- 1 teaspoon soy sauce
- Pinches of salt
- 2 tablespoons cooking oil, plus more for brushing
- 8-cloves of garlic, minced
- ½ bell pepper, cut into thin matchsticks
- 2 large onions, cut into thin matchsticks
- 1 large carrot, cut into thin matchsticks
- 2 cups cabbage, shredded
- 2-inch piece of ginger, grated

1. To prepare the filling: add to a large bowl the carrot, bell pepper, onion, cabbage, ginger, and garlic. Gently add two tablespoons of olive oil in a pan over high heat. Add the filling mixture and stir in salt and a dash of stevia sweetener if you like. Cook for 3-minutes. Add soy sauce, black pepper and mix well.
2. Add green onions, stir and set aside. In a small bowl, combine enough water and cornstarch to make a creamy paste. Fill the rolls with a tablespoon of filling in center of each wrapper and roll tightly, dampening the edges with cornstarch paste to ensure a good seal. Repeat until all wrappers and filling are used. Preheat your air fryer to 350°Fahrenheit. Brush the rolls with oil, and arrange them in the air fryer, and cook them until crisp and golden for about 20-minutes. Halfway through the cook time flip them over.

PER SERVING
Calories: 263 | Total Fat: 11.2g | Carbs: 8.6g | Protein: 8.2g

Coconut Broccoli

Prep Time: 5 minutes | Cook Time: 30 minutes | Serves 4

- 3 tablespoons ghee, melted
- 15 ounces coconut cream
- 2 eggs, whisked
- 2 cups cheddar, grated
- 1 cup parmesan, grated
- 1 tablespoon mustard
- 1 pound broccoli florets
- A pinch of salt and black pepper
- 1 tablespoon parsley, chopped

1. Grease a baking pan that fits the air fryer with the ghee and arrange the broccoli on the bottom. Add the cream, mustard, salt, pepper and the eggs and toss.
2. Sprinkle the cheese on top, put the pan in the air fryer and cook at 380 degrees F for 30 minutes. Divide between plates and serve.

PER SERVING
Calories: 244 | Fat: 12g | Fiber: 3g | Carbs: 5g | Protein: 12g

Zucchini and Squash Mix

Prep Time: 15 minutes | Cook Time: 12 minutes | Serves 4

- 10 oz Kabocha squash
- ½ zucchini, chopped
- 3 spring onions, chopped
- 1 teaspoon dried thyme
- 2 teaspoons ghee
- 1 teaspoon salt
- 1 teaspoon ground turmeric

1. Chop the squash into small cubes and sprinkle with salt and ground turmeric. Put the squash in the bowl, add zucchini, spring onions, dried thyme, and ghee. Shake the vegetables gently.
2. Preheat the air fryer to 400F. Put the vegetable mixture in the air fryer and cook for 12 minutes. Shake the vegetables after 6 minutes of cooking to avoid burning.

PER SERVING
Calories: 45 | Fat: 1.8g | Fiber: 1.3g | Carbs: 6.8g | Protein: 1.1g

Broccoli and Cranberries Mix
Prep Time: 5 minutes | Cook Time: 25 minutes | Serves 4

- 1 broccoli head, florets separated
- 2 shallots, chopped
- A pinch of salt and black pepper
- ½ cup cranberries
- ½ cup almonds, chopped
- 6 bacon slices, cooked and crumbled
- 3 tablespoons balsamic vinegar

1. In a pan that fits the air fryer, combine the broccoli with the rest of the ingredients and toss. Put the pan in the air fryer and cook at 380 degrees F for 25 minutes. Divide between plates and serve.

PER SERVING
Calories: 173 | Fat: 7g | Fiber: 2g | Carbs: 4g | Protein: 8g

Onion Pakora
Prep Time: 2 minutes | Cook Time: 6 minutes | Serves 6

- 1 cup graham flour
- ¼ teaspoon turmeric powder
- Salt to taste
- 1/8 teaspoon chili powder
- ¼ teaspoon carom
- 1 tablespoon fresh coriander, chopped
- 2 green chili peppers, finely chopped
- 4 onions, finely chopped
- 2 teaspoons vegetable oil
- ¼ cup rice flour

1. Combine the flours and oil in a mixing bowl. Add water as needed to create a dough-like consistency. Add peppers, onions, coriander, carom, chili powder, and turmeric.
2. Preheat air fryer to 350°Fahrenheit. Roll vegetable mixture into small balls, add to the fryer and cook for about 6-minutes. Serve with hot sauce!

PER SERVING
Calories: 253 | Total Fat: 12.2g | Carbs: 11.4g | Protein: 7.6g

Prosciutto Asparagus Mix
Prep Time: 5 minutes | Cook Time: 10 minutes | Serves 4

- 2-pounds asparagus, trimmed
- 2 tablespoons avocado oil
- 1 cup Mozzarella cheese, shredded
- 2 oz prosciutto, chopped

1. Mix asparagus with avocado oil and put it in the air fryer.
2. Then top the vegetables with mozzarella and prosciutto.
3. Cook the meal at 400F for 10 minutes.

PER SERVING
Calories: 95 | Fat: 3.2g | Fiber: 5.1g | Carbs: 9.g | Protein: 10.1g

Cheesy Okra
Prep Time: 10 minutes | Cook Time: 10 minutes | Serves 4

- pound okra, trimmed
- ½ cup Monterey Jack cheese, shredded
- 1 teaspoon coconut oil, melted
- 1 teaspoon Italian seasonings

1. Mix okra with coconut oil and Italian seasonings and put in the air fryer.
2. Cook the vegetables for 8 minutes at 380F.
3. Then shake the vegetables and sprinkle them with cheese.
4. Cook the meal for 2 minutes more.

PER SERVING
Calories: 111 | Fat: 6g | Fiber: 3.6g | Carbs: 8.7g | Protein: 5.7g

Garlic Fennel Bulb
Prep Time: 10 minutes | Cook Time: 15 minutes | Serves 2

- 10 oz fennel bulb
- 1 teaspoon avocado oil
- 1 teaspoon garlic powder

1. Chop the fennel bulb roughly and sprinkle with avocado oil and garlic powder.
2. Put the fennel bulb in the air fryer and cook at 375F for 15 minutes.

PER SERVING
Calories: 52 | Fat: 0.6g | Fiber: 4.6g | Carbs: 11.5g | Protein: 2g

Coconut Kohlrabi Mash
Prep Time: 10 minutes | Cook Time: 20 minutes | Serves 6

- 12 oz kohlrabi, chopped
- 2 tablespoons coconut cream
- 1 teaspoon salt
- ½ cup Monterey Jack cheese, shredded
- ¼ cup chicken broth
- ½ teaspoon chili flakes

1. In the air fryer pan mix up kohlrabi, coconut cream, salt, Monterey jack cheese, chicken broth, and chili flakes. Then preheat the air fryer to 255F. Cook the meal for 20 minutes.

PER SERVING
Calories: 64 | Fat: 4.2g | Fiber: 2.2g | Carbs: 3.9g | Protein: 3.6g

Dijon Mustard Asparagus

Prep Time: 5 minutes | Cook Time: 12 minutes | Serves 4

- 1-pound asparagus, trimmed
- 2 tablespoons Dijon mustard
- 1 tablespoon olive oil
- 1 teaspoon lemon juice

1. In the shallow bowl, mix Dijon mustard with olive oil, and lemon juice.
2. Then mix asparagus with mustard mixture and put in the air fryer basket.
3. Cook the meal at 400F for 10 minutes.
4. Then shake the asparagus well and cook it for 2 minutes more.

PER SERVING
Calories: 58 | Fat: 4g | Fiber: 2.7g | Carbs: 4.9g | Protein: 2.8g

Pecan Spinach

Prep Time: 5 minutes | Cook Time: 12 minutes | Serves 4

- 2 cups fresh spinach, chopped
- 2 pecans, chopped
- 1 tablespoon coconut oil
- ½ teaspoon salt
- ½ teaspoon ground coriander

1. Mix spinach with coconut oil, salt, and ground coriander.
2. Put the mixture in the air fryer.
3. Add pecans and cook the meal at 350F for 12 minutes.

PER SERVING
Calories: 82 | Fat: 8.5g | Fiber: 1.1g | Carbs: 1.5g | Protein: 1.2g

Chapter 10
Desserts and Staples

Air-Fried Pineapple in Macadamia Batter
Prep Time: 5 minutes | Cook Time: 7 minutes | Serves 8

- 2 cups pineapple peeled and sliced
- ½ cup macadamia nuts, ground
- ¾ cup almond flour
- ¼ cup cornstarch flour
- ½ teaspoon nutmeg, grated
- ½ teaspoon vanilla extract
- 1 teaspoon orange extract
- ¼ teaspoon salt
- ½ teaspoon baking powder
- ½ teaspoon baking soda
- 2 tablespoons Truvia
- 1 1/3 cups milk
- 2 tablespoons coconut oil

1. To make batter combine all the ingredients, except for pineapple, in a large mixing bowl.
2. Preheat your air-fryer to 380°Fahrenheit. Dip the slices of pineapple into batter. Air-fry for 7-minutes or until golden.

PER SERVING
Calories: 206 | Total Fat: 10.3g | Carbs: 26.6g | Protein: 3.8g

Coconut Prune Cookies
Prep Time: 5 minutes | Cook Time: 20 minutes | Serves 10

- ½ teaspoon baking soda
- ½ teaspoon baking powder
- ½ teaspoon orange zest
- 1 teaspoon vanilla paste
- 1/3 teaspoon ground cinnamon
- 1 stick butter, softened
- 1 ½ cups almond flour
- 2 tablespoons Truvia for baking
- 1/3 cup prunes, chopped
- 1/3 coconut, shredded

1. Mix the butter with Truvia until mixture becomes fluffy; sift in the flour and add baking powder, as well as baking soda. Add the remaining ingredients and combine well. Knead the dough and transfer it to the fridge for 20-minutes.
2. To finish, shape the chilled dough into bite-size balls; arrange the balls on a baking dish and gently flatten them with the back of a spoon. Air-fry for 20-minutes at 315°Fahrenheit.

PER SERVING
Calories: 227 | Total Fat: 10.3g | Carbs: 32.5g | Protein: 2.3g

Delicious Clafoutis
Prep Time: 5 minutes | Cook Time: 25 minutes | Serves 6

- ¼ teaspoon nutmeg, grated
- ½ teaspoon crystalized ginger
- 1/3 teaspoon ground cinnamon
- ½ teaspoon baking soda
- ½ teaspoon baking powder
- 2 tablespoons Truvia for baking
- ½ cup coconut cream
- ¾ cup coconut milk
- 3 eggs, whisked
- 4 medium-sized pears, cored and sliced
- 1 ½ cups plums, pitted
- ¾ cup almond flour

1. Lightly grease 2 mini pie pans using a non-stick cooking spray. Lay the plums and pears on the bottom of pie pans. In a saucepan that is preheated over medium heat, warm the cream along with the coconut milk until thoroughly heated. Remove the pan from heat; mix in the flour along with baking soda and baking powder.
2. In a bowl, mix the eggs, Truvia, spices until the mixture is creamy. Add the creamy milk mixture. Carefully spread this mixture over your fruit in pans. Bake at 320°Fahrenheit for 25-minutes.

PER SERVING
Calories: 354 | Total Fat: 9.6g | Carbs: 66.6g | Protein: 6.2g

Butter Donuts
Prep Time: 5 minutes | Cook Time: 15 minutes | Serves 4

- 8 ounces coconut flour
- 2 tablespoons stevia
- 1 egg, whisked
- 2 and ½ tablespoons butter, melted
- 4 ounces coconut milk
- 1 teaspoon baking powder

1. In a bowl, mix all the ingredients and whisk well. Shape donuts from this mix, place them in your air fryer's basket and cook at 370 degrees F for 15 minutes. Serve warm.

PER SERVING
Calories: 190 | Fat: 12g | Fiber: 1g | Carbs: 4g | Protein: 6g

Cinnamon Donuts
Prep Time: 20 minutes | Cook Time: 6 minutes | Serves 4

- 1 teaspoon ground cardamom
- ½ teaspoon ground cinnamon
- ½ teaspoon baking powder
- ½ cup coconut flour
- 1 tablespoon Erythritol
- 1 egg, beaten
- 1 tablespoon butter, softened
- ¼ teaspoon salt
- Cooking spray

1. Preheat the air fryer to 355F. In the shallow bowl mix up ground cinnamon, ground cardamom, and Erythritol. After this, in the separated bowl mix up coconut flour, baking powder, egg, salt, and butter. Knead the non-sticky dough. Add more coconut flour if needed. Then roll up the dough and make 4 donuts with the help of the donut cutter. After this, coat every donut in the cardamom mixture. Let the donuts rest for 10 minutes in a warm place.
2. Spray the air fryer with cooking spray. Place the donuts in the air fryer basket in one layer and cook them for 6 minutes or until they are golden brown. Sprinkle the hot cooked donuts with the remaining cardamom mixture.

PER SERVING
Calories: 114 | Fat: 6.5g | Fiber: 6.3g | Carbs: 10g | Protein: 4.5g

Almond Donuts
Prep Time: 15 minutes | Cook Time: 14 minutes | Serves 6

- 8 ounces almond flour
- 2 tablespoons Erythritol
- 1 egg, beaten
- 2 tablespoons almond butter, softened
- 4 ounces heavy cream
- 1 teaspoon baking powder

1. In the mixing bowl, mix almond flour, Erythritol, egg, almond butter, heavy cream, and baking powder. Knead the dough.
2. Roll up the dough and make the donuts with the help of the cutter.
3. Put the donuts in the air fryer basket and cook at 365F for 7 minutes per side.

PER SERVING
Calories: 323 | Fat: 29.4g | Fiber: 4.6g | Carbs: 10g | Protein: 10.5g

Vanilla Pie
Prep Time: 10 minutes | Cook Time: 40 minutes | Serves 8

- ½ cup coconut cream
- 3 eggs, beaten
- 1 tablespoon vanilla extract
- 1 teaspoon baking powder
- 3 tablespoons swerve
- 1 cup coconut flour
- 1 tablespoon coconut oil, melted

1. Mix coconut cream with eggs, vanilla extract, baking powder, swerve, coconut flour, and coconut oil.
2. Then transfer the mixture in the air fryer basket and flatten it gently.
3. Cook the pie at 355F for 40 minutes.

PER SERVING
Calories: 139 | Fat: 8.9g | Fiber: 5.3g | Carbs: 9.5g | Protein: 4.4g

Creamy Nutmeg Cake
Prep Time: 20 minutes | Cook Time: 40 minutes | Serves 8

- ½ cup heavy cream
- 3 eggs, beaten
- 3 tablespoons cocoa powder
- 1 teaspoon vanilla extract
- 1 teaspoon baking powder
- 3 tablespoons Erythritol
- 1 cup almond flour
- ¼ teaspoon ground nutmeg
- 1 tablespoon avocado oil
- 1 teaspoon Splenda

1. Mix up heavy cream and eggs in the bowl. Add cocoa powder and stir the liquid until it is smooth. After this, add vanilla extract, baking powder, Erythritol, almond flour, ground nutmeg, and avocado oil. Whisk the mixture gently and pour it in the cake mold. Then cover the cake with foil. Secure the edges of the foil. Then pierce the foil with the help of the toothpick.
2. Preheat the air fryer to 360F. Put the cake mold in the air fryer and cook it for 40 minutes. When the cake is cooked, remove it from the air fryer and cool completely. Remove the cake from the mold and them sprinkle with Splenda.

PER SERVING
Calories: 81 | Fat: 6.7g | Fiber: 1.1g | Carbs: 3.2g | Protein: 3.4g

Mint Cake

Prep Time: 15 minutes | Cook Time: 9 minutes | Serves 2

- 1 tablespoon cocoa powder
- 2 tablespoons coconut oil, softened
- 2 tablespoons Erythritol
- 1 teaspoon peppermint
- 3 eggs, beaten
- 1 teaspoon spearmint, dried
- 4 teaspoons almond flour
- Cooking spray

1. Preheat the air fryer to 375F. Melt the coconut oil in the microwave oven for 10 seconds. Then add cocoa powder and almond flour in the melted coconut oil. After this, add Erythritol, peppermint, and spearmint. Add eggs and whisk the mixture until smooth.
2. Spray the ramekins with cooking spray and pour the chocolate mixture inside. Then put the ramekins with lava cakes in the preheated air fryer and cook them for 9 minutes. Then remove the cooked lava cakes from the air fryer and let them rest for 5 minutes before serving.

PER SERVING
Calories: 538 | Fat: 48.5g | Fiber: 6.9g | Carbs: 14.1g | Protein: 20.8g

Cranberry Whiskey Brownies

Prep Time: 10 minutes | Cook Time: 35 minutes | Serves 8

- 1 teaspoon pure rum extract
- ¼ teaspoon ground cardamom
- 2 tablespoons Truvia for baking
- 2 eggs plus an egg yolk, whisked
- ½ cup coconut oil
- 3 tablespoons coconut flakes
- ¾ cup almond flour
- 8-ounces white chocolate
- 3 tablespoons whiskey
- 1/3 cup cranberries

1. Microwave white chocolate and coconut oil until melted. Allow mixture to cool at room temperature. Next, combine eggs, Truvia, rum extract, and cardamom, whisk well. Add the rum mixture to the chocolate mixture, stirring in flour and coconut flakes. Mix the cranberries with whiskey let soak for 15-minutes. Fold them into the batter. Press the butter lightly into buttered cake pan.
2. Air-fry for 35-minutes at 340°Fahrenheit. Allow them to cool on a wire rack before serving.

PER SERVING
Calories: 367 | Total Fat: 21.8g | Carbs: 36.4g, Proteins: 6.1g

Vanilla Cookies

Prep Time: 10 minutes | Cook Time: 20 minutes | Serves 12

- 2 eggs, whisked
- 1 tablespoon heavy cream
- ½ cup butter, melted
- 2 teaspoons vanilla extract
- 2 and ¾ cup almond flour
- Cooking spray
- ¼ cup swerve

1. In a bowl, mix all the ingredients except the cooking spray and stir well. Shape 12 balls out of this mix, put them on a baking sheet that fits the air fryer greased with cooking spray and flatten them.
2. Put the baking sheet in the air fryer and cook at 350 degrees F for 20 minutes. Serve the cookies cold.

PER SERVING
Calories: 234 | Fat: 13g | Fiber: 2g | Carbs: 4g | Protein: 7g

Raspberry Tart

Prep Time: 5 minutes | Cook Time: 20 minutes | Serves 8

- 5 egg whites
- 1/3 cup Erythritol
- 1.5 cup coconut flour
- 1 teaspoon lime zest, grated
- 1 teaspoon baking powder
- 1/3 cup coconut oil, melted
- 3 oz raspberries
- Cooking spray

1. Mix eggs with Erythritol, coconut flour, lime zest, baking powder, and coconut oil.
2. Whisk the mixture until smooth.
3. Then spray the air fryer basket with cooking spray and pour the batter inside.
4. Top the batter with raspberries and cook at 360F for 20 minutes.

PER SERVING
Calories: 96 | Fat: 9.2g | Fiber: 0.8g | Carbs: 1.9g | Protein: 2.4g

Nutmeg Donuts
Prep Time: 20 minutes | Cook Time: 6 minutes | Serves 4

- 1 teaspoon ground nutmeg
- ½ teaspoon baking powder
- ½ cup almond flour
- 1 tablespoon Swerve
- 1 egg, beaten
- 1 tablespoon coconut oil, softened
- Cooking spray

1. Spray the air fryer basket with cooking spray from inside.
2. Then mix all remaining ingredients and knead the dough.
3. Make the donuts from the dough and put them in the air fryer.
4. Cook the donuts at 390F for 3 minutes per side.

PER SERVING
Calories: 69 | Fat: 6.4g | Fiber: 0.5g | Carbs: 1.4g | Protein: 2.2g

Soft Turmeric Cookies
Prep Time: 10 minutes | Cook Time: 20 minutes | Serves 12

- 2 eggs, beaten
- 1 tablespoon coconut cream
- 3 tablespoons coconut oil, melted
- 2 teaspoons ground turmeric
- 1 teaspoon vanilla extract
- 2.5 cup coconut flour
- 2 tablespoons Erythritol

1. Mix all ingredients in the mixing bowl.
2. Knead the dough and make the cookies using the cutter.
3. Put the cookies in the air fryer basket and cook at 350F for 20 minutes.

PER SERVING
Calories: 147 | Fat: 17g | Fiber: 10.1g | Carbs: 17.6g | Protein: 4.3g

Coconut Hand Pies
Prep Time: 20 minutes | Cook Time: 26 minutes | Serves 6

- 8 oz coconut flour
- 1 teaspoon vanilla extract
- 2 tablespoons Swerve
- 2 eggs, beaten
- 1 tablespoon almond butter, melted
- 1 tablespoon almond meal
- 2 tablespoons coconut shred
- Cooking spray

1. Mix coconut flour with vanilla extract, Swerve, eggs, almond butter, and almond meal.
2. Knead the dough and roll it up.
3. Cut the dough into squares and sprinkle with coconut shred.
4. Fold the squares into the shape of pies and put in the air fryer basket.
5. Sprinkle the pies with cooking spray and cook at 345F for 13 minutes per side.

PER SERVING
Calories: 128 | Fat: 6.5g | Fiber: 7.1g | Carbs: 11.7g | Protein: 5.1g

Appendix 1 Measurement Conversion Chart

Volume Equivalents (Dry)	
US STANDARD	METRIC (APPROXIMATE)
1/8 teaspoon	0.5 mL
1/4 teaspoon	1 mL
1/2 teaspoon	2 mL
3/4 teaspoon	4 mL
1 teaspoon	5 mL
1 tablespoon	15 mL
1/4 cup	59 mL
1/2 cup	118 mL
3/4 cup	177 mL
1 cup	235 mL
2 cups	475 mL
3 cups	700 mL
4 cups	1 L

Volume Equivalents (Liquid)		
US STANDARD	US STANDARD (OUNCES)	METRIC (APPROXIMATE)
2 tablespoons	1 fl.oz.	30 mL
1/4 cup	2 fl.oz.	60 mL
1/2 cup	4 fl.oz.	120 mL
1 cup	8 fl.oz.	240 mL
1 1/2 cup	12 fl.oz.	355 mL
2 cups or 1 pint	16 fl.oz.	475 mL
4 cups or 1 quart	32 fl.oz.	1 L
1 gallon	128 fl.oz.	4 L

Temperatures Equivalents	
FAHRENHEIT(F)	CELSIUS(C) APPROXIMATE)
225 °F	107 °C
250 °F	120 ° °C
275 °F	135 °C
300 °F	150 °C
325 °F	160 °C
350 °F	180 °C
375 °F	190 °C
400 °F	205 °C
425 °F	220 °C
450 °F	235 °C
475 °F	245 °C
500 °F	260 °C

Weight Equivalents	
US STANDARD	METRIC (APPROXIMATE)
1 ounce	28 g
2 ounces	57 g
5 ounces	142 g
10 ounces	284 g
15 ounces	425 g
16 ounces (1 pound)	455 g
1.5 pounds	680 g
2 pounds	907 g

Appendix 2 The Dirty Dozen and Clean Fifteen

The Environmental Working Group (EWG) is a nonprofit, nonpartisan organization dedicated to protecting human health and the environment Its mission is to empower people to live healthier lives in a healthier environment. This organization publishes an annual list of the twelve kinds of produce, in sequence, that have the highest amount of pesticide residue-the Dirty Dozen-as well as a list of the fifteen kinds of produce that have the least amount of pesticide residue-the Clean Fifteen.

THE DIRTY DOZEN	
The 2016 Dirty Dozen includes the following produce. These are considered among the year's most important produce to buy organic:	
Strawberries	Spinach
Apples	Tomatoes
Nectarines	Bell peppers
Peaches	Cherry tomatoes
Celery	Cucumbers
Grapes	Kale/collard greens
Cherries	Hot peppers
The Dirty Dozen list contains two additional itemskale/collard greens and hot peppers-because they tend to contain trace levels of highly hazardous pesticides.	

THE CLEAN FIFTEEN	
The least critical to buy organically are the Clean Fifteen list. The following are on the 2016 list:	
Avocados	Papayas
Corn	Kiw
Pineapples	Eggplant
Cabbage	Honeydew
Sweet peas	Grapefruit
Onions	Cantaloupe
Asparagus	Cauliflower
Mangos	
Some of the sweet corn sold in the United States are made from genetically engineered (GE) seedstock. Buy organic varieties of these crops to avoid GE produce.	

Appendix 3 Index

A

all-purpose flour 50, 53
allspice 15
almond 5, 14
ancho chile 10
ancho chile powder 5
apple 9
apple cider vinegar 9
arugula 51
avocado 11

B

bacon 52
balsamic vinegar 7, 12, 52
basil 5, 8, 11, 13
beet 52
bell pepper 50, 51, 53
black beans 50, 51
broccoli 51, 52, 53
buns 52
butter 50

C

canola oil 50, 51, 52
carrot 52, 53
cauliflower 5, 52
cayenne 5, 52
cayenne pepper 52
Cheddar cheese 52
chicken 6
chili powder 50, 51
chipanle pepper 50
chives 5, 6, 52
cinnamon 15
coconut 6
Colby Jack cheese 51
coriander 52
corn 50, 51
corn kernels 50
cumin 5, 10, 15, 50, 51, 52

D

diced panatoes 50
Dijon mustard 7, 12, 13, 51
dry onion powder 52

E

egg 14, 50, 53
enchilada sauce 51

F

fennel seed 53
flour 50, 53
fresh chives 5, 6, 52
fresh cilantro 52
fresh cilantro leaves 52
fresh dill 5
fresh parsley 6, 52
fresh parsley leaves 52

G

garlic 5, 9, 10, 11, 13, 14, 50, 51, 52, 53
garlic powder 8, 9, 52, 53

H

half-and-half 50
hemp seeds 8
honey 9, 51

I

instant rice 51

K

kale 14
kale leaves 14
ketchup 53
kosher salt 5, 10, 15

L

lemon 5, 6, 14, 51, 53
lemon juice 6, 8, 11, 13, 14, 51
lime 9, 12
lime juice 9, 12
lime zest 9, 12

M

maple syrup 7, 12, 53
Marinara Sauce 5
micro greens 52
milk 5, 50
mixed berries 12
Mozzarella 50, 53
Mozzarella cheese 50, 53
mushroom 51, 52
mustard 51, 53
mustard powder 53

N

nutritional yeast 5

O

olive oil 5, 12, 13, 14, 50, 51, 52, 53
onion 5, 50, 51
onion powder 8
oregano 5, 8, 10, 50

P

panatoes 50, 52
paprika 5, 15, 52
Parmesan cheese 51, 53
parsley 6, 52
pesto 52
pink Himalayan salt 5, 7, 8, 11
pizza dough 50, 53
pizza sauce 50
plain coconut yogurt 6
plain Greek yogurt 5
porcini powder 53
potato 53

R

Ranch dressing 52
raw honey 9, 12, 13
red pepper flakes 5, 8, 14, 15, 51, 53
ricotta cheese 53

S

saffron 52
Serrano pepper 53
sugar 10
summer squash 51

T

tahini 5, 8, 9, 11
thyme 50
toasted almonds 14
tomato 5, 50, 52, 53
turmeric 15

U

unsalted butter 50
unsweetened almond milk 5

V

vegetable broth 50
vegetable stock 51

W

white wine 8, 11
wine vinegar 8, 10, 11

Y

yogurt 5, 6

Z

zucchini 50, 51, 52, 53

THELMA J. LANGLEY

Printed in Great Britain
by Amazon